SISTERS IN SCRIPTURE

*Exploring the Relationships
of Biblical Women*

KATHLEEN MacINNIS KICHLINE

Paulist Press
New York/Mahwah, NJ

Cover design by Cindy Dunne
Book design by Lynn Else

Library of Congress Cataloging-in-Publication Data

Kichline, Kathleen MacInnis.
    Sisters in Scripture : exploring the relationships of biblical women /Kathleen MacInnis Kichline.
        p. cm.
    ISBN 978-0-8091-4580-5 (alk. paper)
    1. Women in the Bible. 2. Catholic women—Religious life. 3. Bible—Criticism, interpretation, etc.
I. Title.
    BS575.K525 2009
    220.9′2082—dc22

                                                          2008041056

Published by Paulist Press
997 Macarthur Boulevard
Mahwah, New Jersey 07430

www.paulistpress.com

Printed and bound in the
United States of America

CONTENTS

For the Facilitator

Sisters in Scripture was created in response to the demand from Catholic women to have a scripture study that was made for women and focused on a specific theme. Originally designed and used in a parish, *Sisters in Scripture* has also been successfully used in a home setting. It has been a tool for women who have already been coming together for a long time and it has been the occasion for women from various places to come together for the first time. Some groups have been small enough for all to discuss together; other gatherings have split into small groups. Originally the author taught the section "A Closer Look at the Text" in person. The study has, however, been used on its own, without a resource person or teacher. In that case, the group goes through this closing section, reading a paragraph at a time aloud, one person at a time, pausing, as needed, for discussion.

The Reflection Questions and the sharing on them that occurs in the small group are the heart of this study. The role of the facilitator is important in assuring the comfort of the participants by following the guidelines for sharing. It is also important to model participation by seriously undertaking the between-sessions work on the text. All participants are encouraged to hold one another in prayer throughout the week, but this is a special task of the facilitator.

Although the request for this study came from Catholic women, it has consistently been attended by women from other Christian denominations as well. If women from other traditions are a part of the group, this should be acknowledged at the Introductory Session along with noting that the nature of biblical scholarship is ecumenical. With mutual respect and interest, the ecumenical dimension enriches the discussion and can lead to the building of bridges among women from different traditions. Another application has been for women of several parishes to come together—another kind of important bridge building!

Introductory Session

Hospitality

In advance of participants' arrival, these supplies should be set out:

Sign-in sheet with name, address, phone number, and e-mail

Name tags

Pens and paper

One or two Bibles

Refreshments/coffee, tea

Sign-up sheet for providing refreshments in coming weeks

Each week an environment should be created that conveys this is a special, prayerful place where all are welcome. This can be simply done with a colorful piece of cloth, an open Bible, and a lit candle. Other times flowers or some other seasonal or thematic symbol might be added (e.g., a bowl of water for the Woman at the Well discussion).

Welcome

Greet each person warmly, offer refreshments, and have them create a name tag and fill in the sign-in sheet. Check off the names of those you knew were coming, add the names of those you did not, and, later, note the ones who'd been expected but did not come.

Once everyone is comfortable, begin by having everyone go around to introduce themselves: their name, perhaps their affiliation with the parish or some other personal fact, what previous experience they've had with scripture, and what their hopes are of this study.

Opening Prayer

Thank everyone for sharing and explain that we pray better when we are not strangers to one another. Explain that prayer together, in addition to on our own, is an important part of this scripture study.

Invite participants to get comfortable and center themselves. Some suggestions for prayer:

- Your own spontaneous prayer
- Reading a favorite scripture selection (e.g., Psalm 139)
- Singing a song (e.g., one used at Mass the past Sunday)
- An Our Father or other shared, memorized prayer
- Inviting a participant with the gift for leading prayer to do so (ask this ahead of time)
- Reading the following (or some other prayer you want to share):

> *Good and gracious God, we gather together in your name and thank you for the many paths that have brought us here today. We thank you for your gift of sacred scripture; may we grow in our appreciation of that gift in our time together. We ask the guidance of your Holy Spirit as we consider the meaning of your word in our lives and we ask for the gifts of wisdom, patience, and love as we share our stories with one another. This we ask in Jesus' name. Amen.*

Group Facilitation

Ask the group to turn to *"Sisters in Scripture:* A Scripture Study" (p. 5). Go over the various components:

- Critical look at the text
- Personal and communal application
- Women's experience
- Catholic flavor

You may want to discuss briefly how this matches or does not match the experience and expectations brought by the group members. For example, if someone were coming from a previous study that taught that every word in scripture is literally true, they could be uncomfortable with the "critical look at the text," using the tools of scriptural study. They would need to suspend their previous understanding to enter into the spirit of this study or, perhaps, this study would not be a good fit for them. Or others may express, for example, lack of experience at sharing or praying together. Gentle encouragement should suffice—as well as the "Ten Guidelines for Sharing" section (p. 14).

Ask the group to turn to "Schedule" and "Scripture References" (pp. 11 and 12, respectively). Discuss any potential problems with the schedule (e.g., school holidays, etc.), and consider how to resolve them. If the earlier discussion reveals that not many women have had experience with using the Bible, take time now to show how to look up the references. Time might also be spent on which translations various members are using. How to choose a good translation, if someone wants to purchase a Bible for this study, might also be discussed. (Encourage a study Bible with ample footnotes, if possible.)

Discuss "How To Use This Study" (p. 13). Ask, "What will be the best time/place for you to fit this into your personal schedule?" Encourage women to make a commitment to the study. Explain that they will get more out of it themselves, and we are all enriched by what we experience from one another. Give them permission to "slip" from time to time—assure them that we'll carry one another at such times.

Go through the "Ten Guidelines for Sharing" (p. 14). Tell the women that we all share in the task of following these guidelines and helping one another create a safe space for our stories, learnings, and questions.

Briefly review the materials for next week's discussion on Sarah:

- Background
- Reflection Questions
- Sarah's Prayer

Draw special attention to the invitation on the Reflection Questions to write a midrash and to "What Is a Midrash?" (p. 15), as well as to the sample midrashes in the Appendix. Encourage the women to try their hand at it, and let them know that time will be taken each week to share any that are created. As the weeks progress, they will feel more comfortable with giving it a try.

Get sign-ups for refreshments for the next week. Be sure everyone has your phone number. Let them know it's not too late to bring a friend.

Closing Prayer

Explain and practice a "squeeze prayer" to close. This is an excellent way to close all the sessions should you choose to.

Everyone stands and joins hands. The ABCs are:

A = be Audible

B = be Brief

C = be Christ centered

Start the prayer yourself, for example: *"Thank you, Jesus for our time together. I ask you to bless each woman in the week ahead and help her find time in her busy schedule to spend some time with scripture."*

Then, squeeze the hand of the woman next to you who, similarly, voices a short prayer of thanks, request, praise, or contrition and then passes the squeeze along. Anyone can choose, instead, to simply pass the squeeze along wordlessly as well. When the squeeze comes back to you, end with, *"Glory be to the Father, and to the Son, and to the Holy Spirit, Amen."*

SISTERS IN SCRIPTURE:
A SCRIPTURE STUDY

What Makes Sisters in Scripture *a* Scripture Study?

A scripture study contains two elements:

1. A critical look at the text (i.e., using the means of modern research and biblical scholarship tools):

- Historical setting
- Context
- Literary form
- Authorship

In this, we use as a guiding principle what the Church teaches about the use of scripture. Vatican II's Constitution on Divine Revelation, *Dei Verbum*, says:

> Since God speaks in sacred Scripture through men in human fashion, the interpreter of sacred Scripture, in order to see clearly what God wanted to communicate to us, should carefully investigate what meaning the sacred writers really intended, and what God wanted to manifest by means of their words.
>
> Those who search out the intention of the sacred writers must, among other things, have regard for "literary forms." For truth is proposed and expressed in a variety of ways, depending on whether a text is history of one kind or another, or whether its form is that of prophecy, poetry, or some other type of speech. The interpreter must investigate what meaning the sacred writer intended to express and actually expressed in particular circumstances as he used contemporary literary forms in accordance with the situation of his own time and culture. For the correct understanding of what the sacred writer wanted to assert, due attention must be paid to the customary and characteristic styles of perceiving, speaking, and narrating which prevailed at the time of the sacred writer, and to the customs men normally followed at that period in their everyday dealings with one another.

But, since holy Scripture must be read and interpreted according to the same Spirit by whom it was written, no less serious attention must be given to the content and unity of the whole of Scripture, if the meaning of the sacred texts is to be correctly brought to light. (§12)

2. A personal and communal application of what scripture means here and now. Although we certainly want to look at what a story meant at the time it was composed, it is often more important to our faith life to know what the story can mean here and now. Scripture stories are not just about characters or history; they are more about our own lives—what we are being called to do in our lives and in the life of our community. Thus, we will incorporate reflection questions that invite participants to apply the sacred texts to their own lives and then we will share what we learn with one another. All of this will be "hemmed in" with prayer as we study at home and when we gather as a group.

It is our goal to use both the tools of scriptural scholarship and the discipline of prayerful reflection to break open the text for its meaning or meanings. For the scriptural text always holds many layers of possible interpretation. It is not our purpose in this study to look for "right answers" but, rather, to encounter God's word as living and relevant. As scripture scholar Megan McKenna says, "We must begin the readings and the reflections with respect and honor the text, love it, and develop a relationship with it and with others, especially those who disagree with our thoughts about its meanings" (*Leave Her Alone,* p. 6).

What Makes It a Women's Scripture Study?

Women attend; therefore, women's experiences, questions, and concerns drive the search for meaning and application in scripture. There is a natural tendency and dynamic for women in gathering to support one another's lives and faith journeys. We value that second aspect of bible study—application to life experience—and will continually look for ways in which our prayers, relationships, and faith walk can be enriched by the scriptures we encounter.

The subject of our study will not be limited to scriptures about women because all scripture is instructive and life giving. We will, however, look at scripture for those stories, images, and meanings that are related to women's experiences and that might otherwise be overlooked or underdeveloped.

In this first round of scripture studies, we will focus on the relationships between some women whose stories intersect in the Bible. Therefore, we will examine our own relationships as women.

What Makes It a Catholic Women's Scripture Study?

As Catholics, we approach the scriptures with that experience, awareness, and intention. We are informed by our life experiences, our prayer life, and our shared liturgical year and worship. As a parish faith community, we have in common certain incidentals (e.g., having heard a particular song at Mass on Sunday) and a foundational desire to share in realizing the presence of God in our midst as a parish.

That desire can span parish boundaries and bring women together from different parishes as well. It can even bring women together across denominational boundaries. In this era of the common lectionary, Christians of many traditions are sharing the same readings on Sunday mornings, reflecting on the same questions, and being challenged to incorporate the Gospel into their lives.

In terms of biblical scholarship, there is no such thing as a "Catholic" bible study. All the work that has been done in scripture studies since the middle of the twentieth century has been ecumenical in nature. When Pope Pius XII opened up the field and encouraged Catholic scholars in the 1940s, we joined mainline Protestants and Jews in a shared, respectful, exciting venture. For relative newcomers to the field, Catholics quickly made significant contributions through the work of scholars like Raymond E. Brown. Catholic scripture scholars do not represent a school of study as such but, rather, are contributors to the larger field. We will draw upon the work of scripture scholars from throughout the field of studies.

A foundational teaching of the Catholic Church on scripture is most noteworthy: we do not believe that scripture should be interpreted literally. In not taking the words to be literally true as they appear on the page, we are at variance with more fundamentalist Protestant churches. However, we are in alignment and complete agreement with most mainline Protestant churches. Given that the fundamentalist approach to the Bible is prevalent in today's Christian culture and represents a large section of bible studies, there can be confusion around our Catholic, ecumenical approach. We are inspired by our fundamentalist brothers and sisters in their love of and enthusiasm for scripture and hope to grow in that regard as Catholics.

We hope to be free of judgment around others' appropriation of God's word and seek for commonalities whenever possibility. We also seek to be free from literalism and rigidity of interpretation of our own sacred texts of Catholicism.

When we look for and discuss the relevance and meaning of a text, we will draw upon our shared Catholic experience, culture, and imagination. As we believe in the importance of the role of tradition, we will look to it for insight and enrichment, drawing upon our history, saints, writings, and prayers as a resource for understanding.

PLANNING YOUR SESSIONS

Sisters in Scripture is designed so that it can be used in two sessions, one focusing on women from the Old Testament (8 weeks, including the Introductory Session), and another focusing on women from the New Testament (7 weeks, including the Closing Session). These sessions can be offered fall and spring, over two separate years, Lents, summers, or whatever configuration suits your group.

Sisters in Scripture, Part One		**Sisters in Scripture, Part Two**	
I	Introduction	IX	Elizabeth
II	Sarah	X	Mary of Nazareth
III	Hagar	XI	Martha of Bethany
IV	Rebecca	XII	Mary of Bethany
V	Rachel	XIII	Mary Magdalene
VI	Leah	XIV	Woman at the Well
VII	Ruth	XV	Closing Session*
VIII	Naomi		

A Note on the Closing Session: The Closing Session is designed to be a morning, afternoon, or evening of reflection, depending on your group's usual meeting time. The regular meeting time should be extended an extra hour or hour and a half and include a meal together. You may even want to consider meeting in a different location, if available. Be sure to agree well ahead of time when, for how long, and where the Closing Session will take place. Remind participants again in the course of the study to plan on keeping that date.

EVALUATION FORM

At the end of this book is an evaluation form for the course. You may or may not wish to use the evaluation; however, asking the students to complete and return the form may be helpful to you in planning future offerings of this course or sequels to it.

You may choose to photocopy the form from your own book and hand these out, or ask the participants to complete the form in their books and tear out the pages. In either case, explain that each participant is free to answer as few or as many of the questions as she wishes, and that participants are welcome to sign their names or not, as each chooses.

Ideally, you should mention the evaluation form at the final "class" session of the course ("Woman at the Well") and ask participants to return the completed form at the Closing Session.

SCHEDULE

Week	Topic	Date
I	Introductory Session	5/
II	Sarah	5/
III	Hagar	5/
IV	Rebecca	
V	Rachel	
VI	Leah	
VII	Ruth	
VIII	Naomi	
IX	Elizabeth	
X	Mary of Nazareth	
XI	Martha of Bethany	
XII	Mary of Bethany	
XIII	Mary Magdalene	
XIV	Woman at the Well	
XV	Closing Session	

SCRIPTURE REFERENCES

Sarah and Hagar: Genesis 12, 16, 18:1–15, 21:1–20

Rebecca: Genesis 24, 25:19–34, 26:1–11, 27, 28:1–9

Rachel and Leah: Genesis 29—31

Ruth and Naomi: Book of Ruth

Elizabeth and Mary of Nazareth: Luke 1

Martha and Mary of Bethany: Luke 10:38–42; John 11:1–44, 12:1–11

Mary Magdalene: Mark 15:40—16:14; Matthew 27:55—28:10; Luke 8:1–3, 23:44—24:12; John 19:25, 20:1–18

Woman at the Well: John 4:1–42

HOW TO USE THIS STUDY

At Home

The following four movements are suggested for your reading and reflecting on the scriptures. They can be done in four different time frames, in two or three, or all at once. In each case a prayerful attitude is important, aware that you are entering into the word of God and asking the Holy Spirit to guide and enlighten you.

I
Pray
Read assigned scripture
Make notes on questions that come to mind

II
Pray
Read background material
Reread assigned scripture

III
Pray
Respond in written form to Reflection Questions

IV
Pray
Optional—Respond to CHALLENGE question, write a poem or a midrash, or create a picture in a medium of your choosing

In the Group

- Gather, welcome, check-in, get refreshments, and settle in
- For the Opening Prayer, read prayer of that week together
- Group discussion on week's reading/Reflection Questions/share CHALLENGE, midrash
- Read "A Closer Look at the Text" one paragraph at a time, going around group
- Closing Prayer of group's choosing or squeeze prayer

If a group becomes large—ten or more—it is best to break into two small groups for the group discussion and then come together again for the "A Closer Look at the Text" section. Take time first to share with one another any midrash or significant insights.

TEN GUIDELINES FOR SHARING

1. Respect confidentiality: Repeat only your experience of a session— never another person's story, experiences, or feelings.

2. Take time; allow every woman the chance to speak.

   • If you are an introvert, challenge yourself to speak up at least once or twice at every gathering.
   • If you are an extrovert, do not share more than two or three times until everyone has had the chance to speak.

3. Speak only for yourself, drawing on your own experiences, feelings, insights, and questions.

4. Use "I" statements. (Use phrases that are specific to you and not universal. Avoid, "People always feel angry when that happens." Say, instead, "It makes me feel angry when that happens to me.")

5. Suspend your sense of certainty.

6. Ask for what you need.

7. Give other people the space or time they need to experience their feelings.

8. Avoid "should." Do not give advice or problem solve.

9. "Thank you" is an appropriate response.

10. Silence is okay.

WHAT IS A MIDRASH?

Each session of *Sisters in Scripture* invites you to create a midrash. In the Jewish tradition, a midrash is a story about a story in the Bible. The belief is that there are a thousand different meanings to every biblical story. One saying goes that the Torah was not written with black ink on white parchment but with black flames upon white flames—that there is just as much truth in the spaces between the flames as there is in the flames. A midrash fills in those holes or gaps like embroidery upon cloth. Often a midrash seeks to answer some question that the story raises—for example, why did Lot's wife turn around? The people who tell such stories are *darshanim,* often rabbis or teachers, and the stories they tell are called midrashes. A midrash recognizes that the best way to understand a story can be to make up a new story about it.

The midrash you create may be an actual story about the story, but can be any way of imaginatively entering the text and creating some way of expressing the truth, the wonder, or the questions that it contains. One of the most common ways is to take on the voice of one of the characters and go from there. It can even be as simple as taking the form of a letter or dialogue.

A medium other than words can also be used. You may be more comfortable with paints, clay, fabric, or music. Any form of expression—maybe even one you've never tried before—would be an appropriate way to represent your encounter with the text. We are, after all, dealing with the word of God, living and moving in our lives, and the Holy Spirit, the Source of all creativity. Who knows what we will be inspired to create?

Please see the Appendix for several midrashes actually created by women in a *Sisters in Scripture* group in 2005–06.

Another creative element of *Sisters in Scripture* is the boxed CHALLENGE question at the end of the Reflection Questions. This is not necessarily meant to be shared, unless you choose to do so. It is meant for you to consider personally and try to answer in your own prayer life or journaling.

SARAH

Background

In order to understand the story of Sarah, we need to look at the larger story of her husband, Abraham. Abraham is a giant not only in scripture, in the story of the Hebrew people, and in the history of all three major monotheistic religions, but also in the history of the human race. With Abraham, God breaks through to human consciousness. The Creator of heaven and earth chooses to become known and to enter into a relationship, which is called the covenant. This covenant or sacred, binding, mutual promise is made not only with Abraham but, through Abraham, with his descendants and, through them, with all humanity.

The Jewish theologian Samuel H. Dresner describes it well in his book, *Rachel*:

> Imagine an hourglass wide at the top and bottom, narrowing at the center to a slender passage, and you will have an image of the biblical record of the covenant. The metaphor is apt. For the "top" and the "bottom," history's beginning and end, its first hope and final fulfillment—each universal in scope and embracing all humanity— are joined by a single man, Abraham....The covenant with Abraham is a narrowing to a single person of what was meant from the very first for all humankind. From Abraham, it was to reach, in succession, one family, one people, one land, and in the end of days, all lands and all peoples. A solitary person then stood between what was intended to embrace every human creature at the beginning of the covenant's revelation....
>
> The keeping, then, and transmission of the covenant becomes the central drama of the patriarchal story. The lives and stories of all these people only makes sense within that context. What was bestowed upon them they dare not keep for themselves, lest the dream for all humanity die aborning, what they receive, they are obliged to transmit....The

record of [their] lives can be understood only if we remember that they are meant to be the special vehicles or the receiving and transmitting of the covenant. (pp. 4, 6)

Because the handing down of the covenant from one generation to the next is essential, Sarah's role as wife of Abraham takes center stage; she is the vessel through which all of this will be accomplished. Her barrenness, then, becomes both pivotal and paradoxical. Barrenness is a recurring theme in scripture. In Sarah's case it underscores two important themes: (1) how fragile, tenuous, and precarious is the thread of this promise (and how precious is its fruit); and (2) that only by God's design will all of this come to fulfillment. Abraham and Sarah are helpless to bring that about themselves. God, who initiated the divine encounter with Abraham, remains the primary mover in the human events recorded in scripture.

Sarah, first of the matriarchs, has a primary role in cooperating with God's divine plan to bless Abraham, their family, the resulting people, and, through them, all humankind: "In you all the families of the earth shall be blessed" (Gen 12:3b). From the beginning, the covenant had universal implications. This was frequently lost sight of in the struggle of the Israelite people to survive—often over and against other peoples. But from its first utterance, the covenant was undeniably intended by God to extend, eventually, to all peoples.

How aware or committed was Sarah to Abraham's God? What did she think of all these strange events? These are intriguing questions to bring into our reading.

A word about the ages of Abraham and Sarah: Throughout the Old Testament exceedingly long ages are attributed to people: "Sarah lived one hundred twenty-seven years; this was the length of Sarah's life" (Gen 23:1) and "this is the length of Abraham's life, one hundred seventy-five years" (Gen 25:7). These life spans are slight, however, compared to some of the other characters in the earlier pages of Genesis—Adam lived for 930 years and his son, Cain, lived for 912 years! The earliest stories of Genesis, chapters 1—11, are most prone to this because such longevity was seen in the ancient world as a sign of the superiority of the beginning times. By the time of Abraham and Sarah, their ages are less exaggerated but still not to be seen as accurate. Exact numbers and dates were of little value in these ancient times. Such details were less important than the story or pattern being explained and useful in so far as they underscored the basic message.

We can, however, take it that they are elderly—certainly beyond the child-bearing years, when Sarah says, "After I have grown old, and my husband is old, shall I have pleasure?" (Gen 18:12). Sarah's age, in fact, underscores her barrenness and, thus, highlights God's role in the miraculous gift of Isaac.

REFLECTION QUESTIONS

Scripture readings: Genesis 12, 16, 18:1–15, 21:1–13 *20*

- What questions come to mind as you read Sarah's story? Make a note of them to bring to our next gathering.
- As you read, notice when Sarah is silent and when she speaks. What does this say to you about her personality?
- The larger culture of patriarchy determined many of Sarah's choices. What larger cultural forces determine our choices today?
- Do issues around childbearing still factor largely in women's lives?
- Choose one of the stories in Sarah's life: Sarah's version of the Egyptian sojourn, the three visitors, or the sacrifice of Isaac. Write a midrash on it. (A midrash is a Jewish method of working with scripture. It is a story about a story in the Bible. It is an invitation to render an enhanced retelling of the story that fills in missing details and answers underlying questions in a way that is consistent with the deepest perceived meaning of the text. Sometimes this is accomplished by telling the story from the point of view of a secondary character. A medium other than words can be used.) If you do not actually create something out of one of Sarah's stories, still choose one that is of great interest to you and come prepared to discuss why.
- What do you see as exemplary in the story of Sarah? What might it mean to be a matriarch?
- Name someone who has been a matriarch in your life. What qualities in her inspire you?

CHALLENGE

Looking back on the stories within your own family, what were some of the thorny problems, poor decisions, and consequences of which you are aware? Can you still honor the women who lived them, even with their "feet of clay"? Can you imagine a future scenario in which your daughters and granddaughters or others impacted by your life choices might look back at your life story? How would you want them to judge your heart?

Space for your own reflections

SARAH'S PRAYER

God said to Abraham, "As for Sarai your wife, you shall not call her Sarai, but Sarah shall be her name. I will bless her, and moreover I will give you a son by her. I will bless her, and she shall give rise to nations; kings of peoples shall come from her." (Gen 17:15–16)

God has a purpose for our lives as well. The deepest hopes of our heart spring from the desire God has planted within us. What are the deepest longings of your heart? Where is God in the middle of that? What do you think God is calling you to do? Are there delays, uncertainties? Are you being called to patience or to action?

Lord, we thank you for the Sarahs of our lives, those women who have gone before us and shown us something of what it is like to try and follow you. We thank you that you have invited each of us, as you did Sarah, to follow you into a deeper, more faith-filled way of living.

Help us,
O God of Sarah,
to be faithful to your call in our lives,
especially in those times of barrenness and waiting
when your purpose is no longer clear to us.
God of surprises,
give us the gift of laughter when we are faced with life's unexpected turns
and confronted with our own foolishness.
Gift us with new life out of our emptiness
so that we, like Sarah, will rejoice in your faithfulness
and delight in the wonder of your surprising ways.
Amen.

A CLOSER LOOK AT THE TEXT

In our assignment, we read about the sojourn in Egypt in Genesis 12:10–20. However, if we read Genesis 20, we encounter the same story told somewhat differently. (There is a parallel account a generation later of Isaac and Rebecca told in Gen 26:1–11.) Similarly, we read about the covenant at the beginning of Genesis 12 but if we read Genesis 15, we find another recounting of the promise made between Yahweh and Abraham. What's going on here? Did each of these events happen twice?

Genesis 12:10–20

Now there was a famine in the land. So Abram went down to Egypt to reside there as an alien, for the famine was severe in the land. When he was about to enter Egypt, he said to his wife Sarai, "I know well that you are a woman beautiful in appearance; and when the Egyptians see you, they will say, 'This is his wife'; then they will kill me, but they will let you live. Say you are my sister, so that it may go well with me because of you, and that my life may be spared on your account." When Abram entered Egypt the Egyptians saw that the woman was very beautiful. When the officials of Pharaoh saw her, they praised her to Pharaoh. And the woman was taken into Pharaoh's house. And for her sake he dealt well with Abram; and he had sheep, oxen, male donkeys, male and female slaves, female donkeys, and camels. But the LORD afflicted Pharaoh and his house with great plagues because of Sarai, Abram's wife. So Pharaoh called Abram, and said, "What is this you have done to me? Why did you not tell me that she was your wife? Why did you say, 'She is my sister,' so that I took her for my wife? Now then, here is your wife, take her, and be gone." And Pharaoh gave his men orders concerning him; and they set him on the way, with his wife and all that he had.

Genesis 20:1–18

From there Abraham journeyed toward the region of the Negeb, and settled between Kadesh and Shur. While residing in Gerar as an alien, Abraham said of his wife Sarah, "She is my sister." And King Abimelech of Gerar sent and took Sarah. But God came to Abimelech in a dream by night, and said to him, "You are about to die because of the woman whom you have taken; for she is a married woman." Now Abimelech had not approached her; so he said, "Lord, will you destroy an innocent people? Did he not himself say to me, 'She is my sister'? And she herself said, 'He is my brother.' I did this in the integrity of my heart and the innocence of my hands." Then God said to him in the dream, "Yes, I know that you did this in the integrity of your heart; furthermore it was I who kept you from sinning against me. Therefore I did not let you touch her. Now then, return the man's wife; for he is a prophet, and he will pray for you and you shall live. But if you do not restore her, know that you shall surely die, you and all that are yours." So Abimelech rose early in the morning, and called all his servants and told them all these things; and the men were very much afraid. Then Abimelech called Abraham, and said to him, "What have you done to us? How have I sinned against you, that you have brought such great guilt on me and my kingdom? You have done things to me that ought not to be done." And Abimelech said to Abraham, "What were you thinking of, that you did this thing?" Abraham said, "I did it because I thought, There is no fear of God at all in this place, and they will kill me because of my wife. Besides, she is indeed my sister, the daughter of my father but not the daughter of my mother; and she became my wife. And when God caused me to wander from my father's house, I said to her, 'This is the kindness you must do me: at every place to which we come, say of me, He is my brother.'" Then Abimelech took sheep and oxen, and male and female slaves, and gave them to Abraham, and restored his wife Sarah to him. Abimelech said, "My land is before you; settle where it pleases you." To Sarah he said, "Look, I have given your brother a thousand pieces of silver; it is your exoneration before all who are with you; you are completely vindicated." Then Abraham prayed to God; and God healed Abimelech, and also healed his wife and female slaves so that they bore children. For the Lord had closed fast all the wombs of the house of Abimelech because of Sarah, Abraham's wife.

The first story in Genesis 12, the sojourn in Egypt, was part of our reading this week. In the second account from Genesis 20, the journey into the Negeb, we note some differences.

	Genesis 12	Genesis 20
Where	Egypt	Negeb desert
Who	Pharaoh	Abimelech
Names	Abram, Sarai	Abraham, Sarah
Reason	Kill Abram for Sarai's beauty	Kill Abraham for Sarah; no fear of God
Happened	Not known	Sarah untouched
Punishment	Severe plagues	Life threatened, wombs closed
Truth revealed	Not known	God speaks in dream
Result	Abram prospers	Abraham prospers

Genesis 20 makes it very clear that Sarah was not touched by Abimelech; there is no information or reassurance one way or the other in Genesis 12. Genesis 12 refers to severe plagues that struck Pharaoh and his household; Genesis 20 is more specific— all the wombs of wife and maidservants had been closed, and Abimelech's life is threatened. In the first account it is unclear how Pharaoh knew of the deception. The plagues were seen as punishment for a transgression and pharaoh came to understand that the transgression was taking Sarai into his household. In the second account, Abimelech has a dream and is informed by God, in no uncertain terms, what has transpired. In both stories, the duped rulers are horrified. Their concern is not about the deception or about Sarah's honor, but that they might have unwittingly taken something that belonged to another. Sarah was, after all, Abraham's property. The consequences of transgressing that were serious no matter what gods were served. In both versions, in the end, Abram/Abraham prospers from the encounter.

Now, let's compare the two covenant accounts:

Genesis 12:1–3
Now the LORD said to Abram, "Go from your country and your kindred and your father's house to the land that I will show you. I will

make of you a great nation, and I will bless you, and make your name great, so that you will be a blessing. I will bless those who bless you, and the one who curses you I will curse; and in you all the families of the earth shall be blessed."

Genesis 15:1–12, 17–18

After these things the word of the LORD came to Abram in a vision, "Do not be afraid, Abram, I am your shield; your reward shall be very great." But Abram said, "O Lord GOD, what will you give me, for I continue childless, and the heir of my house is Eliezer of Damascus?" And Abram said, "You have given me no offspring, and so a slave born in my house is to be my heir." But the word of the LORD came to him, "This man shall not be your heir; no one but your very own issue shall be your heir." He brought him outside and said, "Look toward heaven and count the stars, if you are able to count them." Then he said to him, "So shall your descendants be." And he believed the LORD; and the LORD reckoned it to him as righteousness. Then he said to him, "I am the LORD who brought you from Ur of the Chaldeans, to give you this land to possess." But he said, "O Lord GOD, how am I to know that I shall possess it?" He said to him, "Bring me a heifer three years old, a female goat three years old, a ram three years old, a turtledove, and a young pigeon." He brought him all these and cut them in two, laying each half over against the other; but he did not cut the birds in two. And when birds of prey came down on the carcasses, Abram drove them away. As the sun was going down, a deep sleep fell upon Abram, and a deep and terrifying darkness descended upon him....When the sun had gone down and it was dark, a smoking fire pot and a flaming torch passed between these pieces. On that day the LORD made a covenant with Abram, saying, "To your descendants I give this land, from the river of Egypt to the great river, the river Euphrates."

The first account is obviously shorter and less detailed than the second. We also see a different emphasis. In the first covenant account, Genesis 12:1–3, the promise is clearly linked to the call to journey to a new land that will be for Abraham and his descendants: "The LORD appeared to Abram and said, 'To your descendants I will give this land'" (Gen 12:7). In Genesis 15 there is much more concern about the descendants who will inherit the promise because Abraham and Sarah are still childless. So comes the reassuring promise of progeny, "Look towards heaven and count the stars, if you are able to count them....So shall your descendants be" (Gen 15:5). In Genesis 15, Abraham falls into a trance and we have the mysterious ritual recounted wherein the various animals are halved and the smoking brazier and flaming torch pass between them. There is definitely a different "feel" in the two accounts.

Throughout the Bible, there are examples of stories being told in several varying forms. (Consider the two very different accounts of creation in Genesis 1 and Genesis 2.) Biblical scholars have studied these and come to identify these various strands. It is important to understand that these stories existed long before they were written down and were retold from generation to generation orally because these were not a literate people. When the stories were written down many centuries after their origin (many during the Babylonian Exile in the sixth century BC), the various strands were all woven together to create the existing text. Weaving is an apt metaphor for how the scriptures were put together, as varying stories were not combined into one version but rather laid alongside one another within the larger whole.

Scripture scholars have come to identify four major strands in the Hebrew scriptures: the Yahwist, the Elohist, the Deuteronomist, and the Priestly, frequently denoted by the initials: "J" (for the German version, "Jahweh"), "E," "D," and "P," respectively. In this week's readings we have examples of both the Yahwist and the Elohist. In the following weeks, we will encounter the Deuteronomist (author of Deuteronomy and portions of other texts) and the Priestly strain (the contribution of the priestly editor who compiled the other portions during the Exile and added significant portions as well). Depending on how detailed the notes in your Bible are, you may find reference in the footnotes to which "author" we are dealing with. Author is a relative term because these are stories whose origins do not trace back to one person but rather are told and retold over time by many people.

One of the major ways in which scripture scholars were able to tease out the two different strands of "J" and "E" was by looking at the original Hebrew language and noting what word was used for God. The Yahwist commonly used the word "Yahweh," or more accurately, the initials "YHWH," because the name of God was unutterable. In some Bibles this is translated as the "Lord." The "Elohist" was more apt to use the word "El," a more common Middle Eastern name for God, often translated as "God."

By comparing texts, certain characteristics of the Yahwist strain and the Elohist strain began to be identified. The Yahwist is the older version and almost always shorter, basic, and less detailed. Interestingly, God is also simpler in the Yahwist accounts. God speaks directly to human beings and is more immediate and direct. Recall how in the second creation account of Genesis 2 from "J," God breathes life into clay to form the first human and later walks in the cool of the evening with Adam. The Yahwist almost always stresses God's blessing.

The Elohist, on the other hand, has a more exalted sense of God. Here God speaks in dreams, a frequent occurrence in the "E" tradition, and the fear of the Lord is stressed. The Priestly strain, which also used the word "El" for God, shares some of the Elohist characteristics in having an exalted, more transcendent sense of God. The first creation account in Genesis 1 is from "P" and features a powerful God who has only to speak from afar to make things occur.

These clues are enough to help us identify which author we are dealing with in both the covenant account and the Sarah-as-sister account. Genesis 12 is from the Yahwist and is the simpler, more direct account of Abraham and Sarah's encounter with the Pharaoh. In Genesis 20, we encounter the Elohist. Writing later, the Elohist has a more exalted understanding of the importance of Abraham and Sarah and a higher sense of ritual purity—setting them apart. Thus, the Elohist would be the one to assure the reader that Sarah was untouched, but the Yahwist added the detail about the closed wombs of Abimelech's women. As for the two covenant accounts, the simpler, shorter one, again, is from the Yahwist in Genesis 12. Here God speaks directly to Abram. The Elohist, in chapter 15, is much longer. Here God speaks to Abraham in a vision, for God is seen as too exalted to encounter directly and Abraham goes into a trance (remember Abimelech's dream, another "E" story). The Elohist provides mystery and detail in the ritual sacrifice of the animals and the smoking brazier passing between the two halves at sunset.

Looking at these various sources for the text is an example of *source criticism*—analyzing the text to determine the sources that went into its formation. Additionally, a source critic looks to the date, style, setting, and the intent of the source.

Another kind of biblical scholarship is *redaction criticism*—a term related to editing. Redaction criticism examines words very closely for the idiosyncrasies of spelling, comparing it to other words of similar meaning. *Form criticism* would point out that in the spelling changes of Abram to Abraham and Sarai to Sarah, we have the introduction of the letter "H" that is part of the acronym for God's holy, unspeakable name. Thus, it is an indication of how both Abraham and Sarah are now wholly given over to YHWH.

Pretty interesting stuff, this "closer look."

Hagar

Background

The story of Hagar is puzzling and troubling to read, particularly in the context of our study—women in relationship. In addition to the difference in the status of Sarah and Hagar as mistress and servant, other stresses are at work in the story—domestic violence, betrayal, sexual exploitation, jealousy, surrogate motherhood, exile, and abandonment.

Hagar, an Egyptian, may have been one of the female slaves that Abram acquired in the Egyptian sojourn in Genesis 12. As such, she would be from a different ethnicity, but it would be a mistake to read overtones of the racial tensions that typify our modern American society into this story. Racism, as we know it today, did not exist in the ancient world. Slavery was a fact of life but was not linked to racial identity. Note that Abraham's descendants become the slaves of the Egyptians within several generations.

Slavery was common throughout the ancient Eastern culture and is referred to frequently in the Bible with many laws about how slaves can and cannot be treated. These scriptural prohibitions provided for a humane, fair practice but did not condemn slavery. Later, of course, this became problematic in the era of American slavery when the Bible was used to support its institutionalization. We see examples in scripture of how slaves were obtained: as captives from war (particularly virgin women [Num 31:7–32]); as families of men, women, and children to pay off their debt (Lev 25:39); purchased from others because they were considered property (Lev 25:44); and as volunteers when, for example, a male slave forsakes freedom to stay with a beloved wife slave (Exod 21:2–6).

Women, whether slaves or not, had no sexual rights in the ancient world. Hagar was Sarah's slave, not Abraham's. As such, she was not acquired to be sexually available. She was not a concubine but, rather, a household slave, a handmaid to her mistress, Sarah. The desperation of barrenness drove Sarah to the decision to "have sons through" Hagar. Children were not only the guarantee of social standing; a child, in this case, was pivotal to keeping alive the promise of the covenant.

Because Hagar was Sarah's possession, so also would her children be. Outrageous as that sounds today, such a solution to the problem was logical and acceptable in the ancient Middle East. The complications that arise are not far removed from today's headlines over surrogate motherhood battles.

Whatever relationship Sarah and Hagar had before the pregnancy, it quickly becomes volatile once Hagar is pregnant with Abraham's child, a child she had no choice in conceiving. She is so abused by Sarah, with Abraham's tacit approval, that she runs away. Her encounter in the desert with the angel of the Lord is both hopeful and troubling. God hears and responds to the plight of this oppressed, marginalized woman. But God also has her return to the place of her mistreatment.

Hagar is, most assuredly, in a dreadful situation. Without choice, without a voice, exiled from all that is familiar and driven by fear to leave all that she has come to know, an amazing thing happens to her—a personal encounter with God who intervenes to save her. Despite her lowly status, Hagar is the first person in the Bible, not just the first woman, who is visited by a divine messenger, the angel of the Lord. She is the first woman to receive the divine promise of descendants, the first woman in the patriarchal story to give birth, and her child becomes the father of a great nation. Additionally, she is the only biblical character to give to God a name, the God of Vision, the "God who sees me."

In giving God the name of the "God who sees me," Hagar speaks for all the unseen, lowly women of the world, even today. Although they may not actually be slaves, many women are without power, protection, voice, or autonomy.

The story of Sarah and Hagar compels us to look at the relationship between women of privilege and women who are marginalized. On a global scale, the very fact that we are educated and can read this study means that we are privileged compared to most of the world. What thought, if any, do we give to women in third-world nations whose resources are a slight fraction of our own? How do we relate to women who serve us, whether they are in public places such as restaurants, nail salons, or stores, or in our own homes as domestics or gardeners? In what ways have we ourselves experienced being disempowered or voiceless? What has that taught us?

The story of Hagar and Ishmael is shared by the Jews and the Muslims. Both religions claim Abraham as their father through the two different sons, Isaac and Ishmael. Judaism and Islam each recount the details somewhat differently. The Muslims, for instance, see Ishmael's first-born status as superior to Isaac's status as son of wife Sarah. They still visit and venerate the well that Hagar discovered. Though the details differ, how remarkable that this story has survived so many centuries and that it continues to inspire millions in three major world religions to this very day.

REFLECTION QUESTIONS

Scripture readings: Genesis 16, 21:1–20

- What questions come to mind as you read Hagar's story? Make a note of them to bring to our next gathering.
- With whom do you identify, Sarah or Hagar? Why? In our culture are we women of privilege or women on the margins? How do we relate to women in the other position?
- Imagine a scenario with the roles reversed.
- Was Hagar a victim of Sarah's abuse? Was Sarah also a victim? What role did patriarchy play in the story?
- What are some of the admirable qualities that you can identify in Hagar?
- Is there a specific situation in your life that mirrors the disparity of roles in the Sarah/Hagar story? How might you enter that situation differently?
- Choose one of the events in the Sarah/Hagar relationship. Write a midrash on it as one of the two women (or as Abraham or one of the two sons).
- Christianity, Judaism, and Islam all claim Abraham as their father. Islam traces its roots back to Ishmael, the son of Hagar. What challenges or hopes do you see in this?

CHALLENGE

How might reconciliation have played a role in the Sarah/Hagar story? Was that possible in that setting? What foundational changes might have to take place in the setting of this story, in the relationships of world religions, or in systemic problems in your own life for reconciliation to happen? How does the Christian imperative to forgive find meaning?

Space for your own reflections

HAGAR'S PRAYER

The angel of the LORD found her by a spring of water in the wilderness, the spring on the way to Shur...So she named the LORD who spoke to her, "You are El-roi"; for she said, "Have I really seen God and remained alive after seeing him?" (Gen 16:7, 13)

God knows and calls each of us by name. God also calls each of us to answer the deeper questions in life—questions like "where have you come from?" and "where are you going?" Like Hagar, we can experience God in times of extreme need, confusion, pain, or anxiety. It is then that God finds us. How shall we respond to this God who breaks into our lives, by what name shall we call him? What do we do with the sometimes confusing requests that God makes of us? Can we trust that God still has more planned for us?

Find us,
O God of Hagar,
wherever our fear bids us to hide.
Call us by our name and reveal to us in that naming moment
your saving, compassionate presence.
El-roi, living God who sees us,
give us the courage of Hagar to trust that you will bring to completion
the promises you have made in our lives;
give us such confidence in your care for us
that we will call you by name;
we will claim you as our own, our God.
Amen.

A CLOSER LOOK AT THE TEXT

Let's take a closer look at what we learned last week about source criticism (analyzing the text to determine the sources that went into its formation). Here are the specifics of the two accounts in Genesis of Hagar's flight into the desert.

	Genesis 16:6–16— Yahwist	Genesis 21:9–21— Elohist
When	Hagar is pregnant with Ishmael.	Ishmael is a young child.
The problem	Hagar looks on Sarai with contempt.	Ishmael plays with Isaac.
Abraham's response	Abram, "Do to her as you please."	Abraham was greatly distressed.
How Hagar left	Sarai abused her so much she ran away.	Abraham gave her bread and water and sent her and the child away.
Where she went	By a spring of water on the road to Shur	Roamed aimlessly in the wilderness of Beer-sheba
How God intervened	The Lord's messenger found her.	God heard the boy's cry.
The initial call	The messenger asked where she was going.	God's messenger called from heaven.
God's words	"Return to your mistress, and submit to her....I will so greatly multiply your offspring that they cannot be counted for multitude....Now you have conceived and shall bear a son; you shall call him Ishmael,	"What troubles you, Hagar? Do not be afraid; for God has heard the voice of the boy where he is. Come, lift up the boy and hold him fast with your hand, for I
		Continued

Continued	for the Lord has given heed to your affliction. He shall be a wild ass of a man, with his hand against everyone, and everyone's hand against him; and he shall live at odds with all his kin."	will make a great nation of him."
What she did next	She named God El-roi, God of vision.	God opened her eyes to see the well and she let her son drink.
The resolution	Hagar returned to Abraham and bore Ishmael to him.	God was with the boy as he grew up in the wilderness of Paran. Hagar got a wife for her son from her native land of Egypt.

Look for some signature signs of both the Yahwist and the Elohist in their respective accounts. Note that the Yahwist has the messenger of the Lord come to Hagar whereas the Elohist has God hear the cry of the child from afar and sends a messenger in response. We know that the Yahwist has a more immanent sense of God, God-with-us, and will often speak of God in anthropomorphic* terms. The Elohist, on the other hand, portrays the transcendent character of God—God as holy, other, powerful, and distant. The Yahwist paints a colorful picture of family strife and both Sarah and Abraham are seen in an unflattering way. The Elohist has a higher sense of the patriarchs and pictures Abraham differently—reluctant to send Hagar and Ishmael away, only doing so out of obedience to God. The Elohist never has either Sarah or God speak the name of Ishmael; he is only referred to as "the boy" or "the son of the slave woman." The story ends with Ishmael banished for good, leaving the inheritance of the promise and the covenant free to Isaac. The Yahwist does not provide such clear resolution and, in general, is more comfortable with ambiguity.

Are you beginning to develop any impressions or preferences as regards these two authors of Hebrew scripture, the Yahwist and the Elohist?

*Anthropomorphic: "Ascribing human characteristics to a being or thing not human, especially a deity." *Random House Dictionary of the English Language.*

REBECCA

Background

The other women in this scripture study are presented as pairs for us to explore their relationships. Rebecca is presented on her own but within the context of other women—those who preceded her and those who came after her. Her role and story are so pivotal that without them, the experiences of the women who follow her would lose much of their meaning.

Rebecca is one of the four women—along with Sarah, Rachel, and Leah—to be considered as matriarchs, *Ima-[h]ot,* or mothers in Hebrew. They are the primary wives of the three patriarchs, *Avot,* or fathers in Hebrew—Abraham, Isaac, and Jacob. As such they are mothers to all Jewish people and their stories take on epic significance.

Although we refer to these important figures of the Hebrew scriptures as matriarchs and patriarchs, patriarchy was not a biblical invention, nor was it unique to these biblical people. *Webster's College Dictionary* defines patriarchy as:

> A form of social organization in which the father is the head of the family, clan or tribe in which power is held and transferred through males and the principles or philosophy upon which control by male authority is based. It is government, rule, power and domination by men. As such patriarchy is a de facto system of sovereign ownership based on gender.

The stories of these matriarchs and patriarchs take place during a time when all of the surrounding culture was patriarchal. Patriarchy preexisted the Bible and, therefore, permeated both the society and the story. Just as the Bible only records the fact of slavery and does not remark on the right or wrong of it as a sociological phenomenon, so the Bible records patriarchy and its consequences but does not provide commentary on it.

So Rebecca's story, like the other matriarchs, is also that of her husband—in this case, Isaac. Perhaps more than the other matriarchs, Rebecca takes center stage. Isaac's story becomes, to a large extent, Rebecca's story, for she plays a determining role in the life of her son, through whom the covenant promise will be transmitted.

Although Rebecca lives out her married life in a male household, she has early, important connections to both her mother and mother-in-law. Her relationship with her mother is glimpsed briefly in the story of Rebecca's betrothal. Immediately Rebecca runs to tell her mother. The mother accepts the gifts of the betrothal, attempts to delay her daughter's departure, and asks her whether she wants to stay or go.

Although Rebecca never meets her mother-in-law, Sarah, she is sought out after Sarah's death by having a servant return to the tribe of Sarah's relatives. She comes to Isaac in the tent of her deceased mother-in-law and "she became his wife; and he loved her….Isaac was comforted after his mother's death" (Gen 24:67). Rebecca's story is, in many ways, a continuation of Sarah's story. Both women were barren for a long period of time and both spoke out and took the initiative in important decisions affecting their lives.

It is easiest to read Rebecca's story as five major episodes:

- Genesis 24—The lengthy process of her betrothal and the journey to marry Isaac
- Genesis 25:19–34—The pregnancy and birth of the twins, Esau and Jacob
- Genesis 26:1–11—Her being passed off as Isaac's sister to the Philistine king
- Genesis 27—Her conspiring with Jacob to secure Isaac's blessing
- Genesis 28:1–9—Her sending Jacob to her brother Laban for safety and a future wife

All together, this represents a lot of material. You may want to go through this a section at a time—you will find that the questions correspond to each of these five episodes.

REFLECTION QUESTIONS

Scripture readings: Genesis 24, 25:19–34, 26:1–11, 27, 28:1–9

- What questions come to mind as you read Rebecca's story? Make a note of them to bring to our next gathering.
- Episode One: Recall the details of the long story about Rebecca's coming to Isaac: the role of the servant, your first impression of Rebecca, Rebecca's mother, the first meeting between Rebecca and Isaac, Rebecca's wedding night in Sarah's tent (Gen 24). What does all this tell you about the people involved?
- Two: Notice in Rebecca's pregnancy and birth story the recurring themes of barrenness, divine annunciation, and harrowing birth. What does this prefigure about the child(ren) to be born?
- Three: As did his father before him, Isaac passed his wife off as his sister in order to protect himself (and her?). In each case, the woman is an item to be exchanged for safety or wealth. This exposed both Sarah and Rebecca to sexual harassment and, potentially, rape. What does this say about men's attitudes toward women's bodies in that culture? Are men more or less respectful of women's bodies today?
- Four: Rebecca conspires with Jacob to take on the role of the trickster. Recall that during her pregnancy Rebecca was given the message that "the elder shall serve the younger" (Gen 25:23), that Esau showed contempt for his birthright by selling it for a bowl of potage (Gen 25:27–34), and that Esau had brought contention into the home in his marriage choice (Gen 26:34–35). Rebecca took on the role of determining which son would inherit the promise. To what extent was she motivated by favoritism? Or was she more in touch with which son was better suited for the task of keeping and passing on the covenant? Do you find Rebecca's deception reprehensible, understandable, or laudable? Why?
- Five: In sending her son away, Rebecca will never see him again but she assures his safety, makes certain that he will not marry a Canaanite (presumably one who would not value the covenant), and sets in motion events that will determine the future. Does this remind you of any other women in similar situations? Can you think of motives strong enough to prompt a similar action by yourself?

CHALLENGE

Rebecca is a woman who takes matters into her own hands. In so doing she affects the lives of all those around her. Can you think of a similar woman in your family story? Does the story of Rebecca make you think/feel differently about her? Rebecca went into her dead mother-in-law's tent and inherited much of her life as well. What similar patterns exist in your own story? Does knowing Rebecca's story help or complicate your feelings on such patterns?

Or write a midrash—a story or a poem—or draw or paint a picture from part of Rebecca's life.

Space for your own reflections

REBECCA'S PRAYER

And the LORD said to her, "Two nations are in your womb, and two peoples born of you shall be divided; the one shall be stronger than the other, the elder shall serve the younger." (Gen 25:23)

Rebecca becomes the mother of Israel (Jacob's later name). She is the first woman in scripture to have a difficult pregnancy. In her pain, she cries to God and God responds to her directly. The knowledge that she receives is both wondrous—she will bear two sons—and troubling—they will be at enmity with each other. She is then in the painful position of watching that rivalry play itself out in the family. She also seems to have taken on the task of being the one to provide that the covenant is transmitted according to her understanding of God's will.

Help us,
O God of Rebecca,
as we contend with family struggles.
We call out to you in our pain and await your faithful answer.
Aware that we ourselves sometimes enter into the fray and are more a
*   cause than a cure to the problem,*
we ask your forgiveness and guidance.
Help us reflect on your divine purpose for our lives
that we might become more aware of your saving action in our story.
We thank you for those who have gone before us and
have shown us something of what it means to love and to follow your way.
We ask your blessing on all who shall come after us that they too will come
*   to know you as their God and value the faith they have received.*
Amen.

A CLOSER LOOK AT THE TEXT

In the last two sessions we have used source criticism as our tool of biblical study: that is, we looked to identify the source of the author(s) of the text. Another tool of biblical study is *form criticism*. Form criticism arises from the awareness that what we are looking at existed first in oral form over a long period of time before it was written down. We try to find out as much about that as we can about the origins of a particular story or piece of scripture—a *pericope (a selection or extract from a larger written piece)*. First we look to see in what form the pericope exists. Is it a saga, a letter, a genealogy? Then we try to determine the setting of the community or group responsible for its development and transmission. Scripture scholars refer to this as the *Sitz-im-Leben* or setting in life (from the original German phrase used by scholars—most early scripture scholars were German). We look at the geographical setting and the social, economic, religious, and political forces that were in effect in a particular *Sitz-im-Leben* to learn as much as we can about their influence. Then we try to identify the purpose of a particular pericope. What was its original purpose in that *Sitz-im-Leben* and what is its purpose now within the larger work? Form criticism may also study the process by which the creation and tradition of a particular tradition takes place. It will look at the development and style of writing and the oral dynamics (e.g., folk stories).

In the Background sections already presented, we took a look at slavery and at patriarchy. In so doing, we were looking at the social setting or *Sitz-im-Leben* of these stories. Such consideration is essential to realizing the real differences that exist between our own time and the time we are reading about in these scripture stories. To take these ancient stories and try to apply them directly to our own time is a misappropriation of the scripture and overlooks the larger question of purpose both then and now.

The purpose of these chapters of Genesis is to tell the story of how, and underscore the importance of why, the transmission of the covenant was effected from generation to generation. This focus helps us gain insights on the text. As Jewish theologian Samuel H. Dresner says in his book *Rachel*:

> The transmission of the covenant takes precedence over all else, even to the point of violating hallowed custom. A case in point is the law of primogeniture, which declares that special rights belong to the first-born male (Deut 21:16–18). But neither Isaac, his son Jacob, Jacob's

son Joseph, nor Joseph's son Ephraim is firstborn. The firstborn are, respectively, Ishmael, Esau, Reuben, and Manasseh. Yet the former and not the latter receive the birthright. The law is clear, but it is set aside for the simple reason that these firstborn sons are not deemed worthy of being entrusted with the task of receiving and handing down the covenant—Esau because he *despised* the birthright (Gen 25:34); Reuben because he "defiled his father's bed" (Chron 5:1). A distinction is clearly made between the biological firstborn and the recipient of the "birthright," usually bestowed through the parental blessing. How to supplant the order of birth and strength with the order of merit is the challenge that each of the patriarchal families faces. (p. 5)

Given the primary importance of the covenant, what happens when you have the pairing of a couple like Isaac and Rebecca where the woman is clearly the more action oriented? Isaac waits for a wife; Rebecca travels. She decides, as did Abraham, to leave her homeland and go to a place she has not seen before. Like Abraham, she is the one who receives a promise from Yahweh about her offspring. It may even be that it was Rebecca, more than Isaac, who had the stronger, clearer sense of how the covenant should be kept alive. Was her intervention in the blessing a case of maternal favoritism or did she recognize that Jacob was the son who should inherit the blessing and who would cherish the covenant?

As the family patriarch, Isaac clearly had the authority to make decisions and expect obedience but Rebecca, nevertheless, has power in this story. She is young and nimble while Isaac is feeble, old, and bedridden. She is more aware of the circumstances in their family and, presumably, more aware of the larger situation and complexities. So, she also has knowledge. That knowledge may even include a sense of whom God has chosen. Lastly, she has the will. She takes it upon herself to act and takes upon herself all of the inherent danger: "Let your curse be on me, my son" (Gen 27:13), she tells Jacob when he, out of fear, protests her strategy. Rebecca is clearly the link between the two generations. Her choices and actions set the stage for all that follows and assure that the covenant is kept alive.

RACHEL

Background

Rachel and Jacob get off to a wildly romantic start. Just as his mother first met the servant of his father at a well, so does Jacob happen upon Rachel. There the similarity ends. Unlike Isaac's emissary, Jacob has no rings or bracelets to offer; he has no home to bring a bride. Samuel Dresner observes: "All he could give was himself: spontaneity, vigor, virility, an act of generosity, and an outburst of love" (*Rachel*, p. 30). "Jacob went up and rolled the stone from the well's mouth, and watered the flock of his mother's brother Laban. Then Jacob kissed Rachel, and wept aloud" (Gen 29:10–11). Apart from the Song of Songs, that kiss is the first and only kiss recorded between a man and a woman in scripture. And what an image is painted of her: "Rachel was graceful and beautiful. Jacob loved Rachel; so he said [to Laban]: 'I will serve you seven years for your younger daughter Rachel'" (Gen 29:17–18).

Their love story would become complicated, however, by the intrigues that pitted two sisters against one another and by the overwhelming tragedy of barrenness. Barrenness was especially painful in a world where the bearing of children fulfilled the first and basic command to humanity, "Be fruitful and multiply" (Gen 1:28). The worth of a woman lay in her ability to bring forth children. They were her social standing in the present generation and provided for her security in the future generation. Rachel's barrenness is, of course, made all the more painful and obvious by her sister's fruitfulness. Alone among the matriarchs, Leah is the mother of many sons. Rachel lives with that comparison on a daily basis. Her sister is not only Jacob's first wife, by deception, but she is also exceedingly fertile.

Where modern sensibilities might find the unquestioning love of her husband to be sufficient, it was not enough for Rachel. She has beauty and she has a husband who loves her but she wants more; she wants children. She is driven to jealousy by her desire and resorts to the supposed aphrodisiac qualities of the mandrake. She blames her husband: "Give me children, or I shall die!" (Gen 30:1). Rachel's barrenness leaves her feeling unfilled in her marriage and as a woman.

REFLECTION QUESTIONS

Scripture readings: Genesis 29—31

- What questions come to mind as you read Rachel's story? Make a note of them to bring to our next gathering.
- Jacob's parents, Isaac and Rebecca, met through an encounter at a well. Jacob meets Rachel at a well. Moses meets his wife Zipporah at a well. Jesus encounters the Samaritan woman at a well. The meeting of a man and a woman at a well sets the stage for a significant meeting. What might be an equivalent setting today?
- Jacob worked seven years to win Rachel but "they seemed to him but a few days because of the love he had for her" (Gen 29:20). Can you think of a modern equivalent to that kind of love story?
- Laban ends up tricking Jacob, who had himself tricked his brother Esau. The ability to "put one over" on another was an admired quality in the Middle East. Later, Rachel puts one over on her father when he comes searching for his stolen idols. Can you think of a contemporary North American quality that might not be shared by other cultures? What other instances of deception are there in this Rachel/Leah story?
- What similarities, if any, do you see in Jacob's deceiving Isaac for the blessing and in his being deceived on his wedding night?
- Rachel goes on to bear two sons and dies in giving birth to the second one, Benjamin. She is revered as a mother to all Israel—her tomb is one of the most visited sites in the Holy Land. She is cited in Jeremiah 31:15 as the Israelites are sent into exile, passing by her tomb, and she weeps for them, her children. What qualities do you see in her that you admire? What traits are problematic?
- Consider writing a midrash: Rachel on Leah's wedding night? Rachel sitting on Laban's household idol? What else?

CHALLENGE

The Bible is silent about Rachel regarding the bridal deception. How do you think she felt? How would you explain her silence? What options, if any, do you think she might have had? In the Hassidic tradition, she was silent for fear that her sister would be put to shame; her silence is credited to her as noble and an example to be followed. Would you agree? What do you think about silence, passivity, complicity, freedom, deception? Can you think of examples from history or your personal life where someone had to make a choice between silence or speaking, passive or active, complicit or disruptive, shackled or free, transparent or deceptive?

Space for your own reflections

RACHEL'S PRAYER

Rachel was graceful and beautiful. Jacob loved Rachel; so he said [to Laban]: "I will serve you seven years for your younger daughter Rachel." (Gen 29:17–18)

When Rachel saw that she bore Jacob no children, she envied her sister; and she said to Jacob, "Give me children, or I shall die!" (Gen 30:1)

Rachel's life is lived with longing—longing and waiting for Jacob, longing for a son and then another. Her immediate assent to fleeing Laban and her defiant theft of his household gods also speak of her longing for a different, better life. Though she dies tragically, her hopes are secured—the love of Jacob and the birth of two sons to receive and pass on the covenant.

Thank you,
God of Rachel,
for the gift of passion,
that unpredictable, divine spark that creates life.
We have felt the leap of that spark within us
and understood that it comes from you,
that it invites us into the life-giving dance of creation.
Thank you for the lives that have sprung from that spark—
our children, our grandchildren,
and the relationships that bind us all to one another.
We have also felt passion fanned into destructive flames of jealousy
when we forget your spark shines within another.
Forgive us and remind us that you, our passionate God,
love each of us beyond reason.
Amen.

A CLOSER LOOK AT THE TEXT

As mentioned last week, one of the first tasks of form criticism is to look at a particular story or pericope to determine what its literary genre is: What type or style of story is it and what is its purpose? In these chapters of Genesis in which the stories of the patriarchs are told, we have a consistent, unique purpose and form of literature. These stories were remembered, told, and retold throughout generations because they were the family stories, the ones that recalled the ancestors. Therefore, they have all the markings of our own colorful family recollections. They are more than that, however, because they explain the background of a whole people, as the descendants of these patriarchs will become.

In earlier chapters of Genesis (1 to 11), yet another purpose or form of literature was in place. Although they appear first in the Bible, they were written down much later, largely by "P" incorporating ancient oral "J" traditions. These chapters span a period of time from creation to about 1900 BC and seek to explain the origin of and questions around human existence. These stories address the big or foundational questions like: Where did life come from? If life is good, why is there evil? Why do we die? As such, they properly belong to a literary form referred to as *myth.* Unfortunately myth is strongly associated, outside of the literary realm, with being imaginary or fictitious. Some years ago, Joseph Campbell wrote *The Power of Myth* and helped popularize an understanding that myth reveals Truth (with a capital "T"—important wisdom but without great concern for truths with a small "t") in which details are often fanciful and not factual. Often myths are *etiological,* which means they explain the cause of something. The tower of Babel, for example, explains the diversity of languages.

The rest of Genesis (chapters 12 to 50) is concerned with telling the patriarchal story. As a literary form this would be a legend or *saga.* It is often challenging for the beginning student of scripture to associate these familiar beloved stories with such literary labels. Lawrence Boadt, in *Reading the Old Testament,* does an admirable job of explaining the term saga for such stories:

> The patriarchal traditions of Abraham, Isaac and Jacob have often been called "legends," half-historical, half-entertaining stories of the past. Because "legend" in English often comes to mean simply fictitious, many scholars today have come to use the term "saga" borrowed from Icelandic family stories of the Middle Ages. Sagas are heroic tales

about the ancestors of a well-known family. They give luster to the family or clan today by telling of the adventures of one or more of its great-great-grandfathers or grandmothers long ago. They often have legendary features, building up the fearless hero almost bigger than real life, and they share some of the characteristics of the epic style: long and very elaborate poems about great heroes who affected the whole course of the nation. Homer's *Iliad* and *Odyssey* and Virgil's *Aeneid* fall in this type of literature.

Sagas show signs of being repeated orally at first, sometimes with more than one version of each story in circulation. Each story-teller can adapt or add themes and local color to his retelling. By the time it is written down, the oral saga may have developed much beyond its earliest form, and two different versions may show quite striking changes from one another. The stories of the patriarchs in Genesis show signs of this. [Example is given here of exactly what we saw in the two stories of Sarah and one of Rebecca being passed off as "sister."]

When we look at these three stories, there would seem to be only one chance in a million that such a coincidence of events could happen three times in two generations, and that both Abraham and King Abimelech could have been so foolish as to fall into the same trap twice in their lives. Originally these three different stories were only *one* story. The same heroic tale about how a patriarch had almost lost his wife to a powerful king was possibly told in three separate cities or towns. One would be Beer-sheba, a city near Gerar associated with Isaac's life, and another would be Hebron, where the story was transferred to Abraham, who was the local hero there. Or else story-tellers in three different tribes each adapted the story to their local audience so that some tribe who lived near Gerar quickly identified the powerful king with Abimelech, while those farther south near the Egyptian border, made the king the Pharaoh of Egypt. In any case, three different versions arose. We cannot know just when and how this happened, but we do know that sagas are preserved and retold only within the group or groups for which they have meaning. Perhaps there was a special story-teller for each tribe which passed on its traditions to his successor. Or perhaps the stories were told at shrines where the priests would learn all the stories and preserve them. While no longer as vital as the oral method of handing on stories, historical legends are preserved in small towns in Europe through the local festivals in honor of a patron saint, now forgotten everywhere but in that village. (pp. 148–49)

Although the purpose in telling such stories was to recall the lives of the ancients, the later crafting and inclusion of the stories into the canon of the Torah served an additional purpose. These people serve as the link between the initial covenanting between Yahweh and Abraham and the later emergence of a whole people who will once again covenant with Yahweh at Sinai under the leadership of Moses.

In the fleshy, fallible stories of these human interactions, the promise continues to be lived out and awareness breaks through in brief and shining moments—for example, Jacob's wrestling with the angel. The powerful connection is made and remade between the story and the reader of scripture that our lives are not so removed from these ancient lives. In the midst of and despite our human dealings, God's plan prevails and, on occasion, breaks through to our awareness.

LEAH

Background

The story of Rachel and Leah centers largely on their producing offspring—sons, in particular, though one daughter of Leah's is mentioned, Dinah. The family tree below may help you keep straight who the various siblings are and to which generation each belongs.

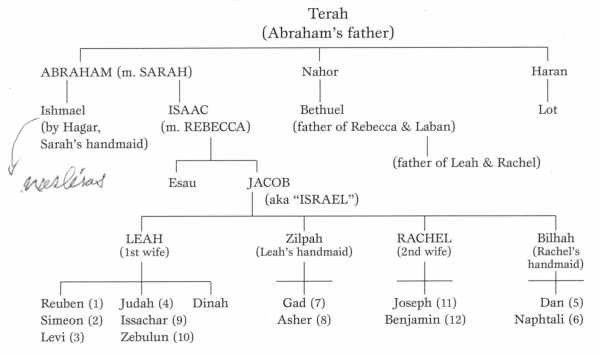

GENESIS FAMILY TREE
Terah
(Abraham's father)

ABRAHAM (m. SARAH)   Nahor   Haran

Ishmael   ISAAC   Bethuel   Lot
(by Hagar,   (m. REBECCA)   (father of Rebecca & Laban)
Sarah's handmaid)

Laban
(father of Leah & Rachel)

Esau   JACOB
(aka "ISRAEL")

LEAH (1st wife)	Zilpah (Leah's handmaid)	RACHEL (2nd wife)	Bilhah (Rachel's handmaid)
Reuben (1) Judah (4) Dinah	Gad (7)	Joseph (11)	Dan (5)
Simeon (2) Issachar (9)	Asher (8)	Benjamin (12)	Naphtali (6)
Levi (3) Zebulun (10)			

49

Proportionately, the stories of Jacob, his wives, and their family comprise a large portion of Genesis and fall into three types. First are the ones around Jacob's relationship with Esau beginning in the womb, through conflict, deception, and separation to eventual reconciliation. Second, there are the family stories about the relationships between Jacob and his wives, Rachel and Leah, and their relationship with one another, and, of course, Laban's relationships with all of them. The third group of stories are *theophanies,* or those that show God: for example, Jacob's ladder (Gen 28:10–22), Jacob wrestles with the angel (Gen 32:22–32), Jacob is renamed Israel (Gen 35:1–15). Although our study will focus on stories from the second group, it is important to remember that the story of God's covenant or promise continues through this family.

There are significant literary parallels in the stories of the two siblings—between Jacob and Esau and between Rachel and Leah. First the younger brother is substituted for the older to receive the blessing, then the older sister is substituted for the younger as the bride—in each case by deception. The theme of trickery runs throughout the story, as when Rachel sits on the household idols to deceive Laban and, in a section not part of our reading, Jacob tricks Laban out of his flocks (Gen 30:25–43).

Jacob and Esau fought for dominance from before birth. Rachel and Leah are pitted against one another by circumstances outside themselves, their brother Laban's scheming to get Jacob's labor for free. The description given of them at the outset suggests, however, that they were noticeably different: "Now Laban had two daughters; the name of the elder was Leah, and the name of the younger was Rachel. Leah's eyes were lovely, and Rachel was graceful and beautiful" (Gen 29:16–17). Rachel caught the eye and, by comparison, Leah did not. Rachel is looked at; Leah looks.

Once they are locked into their shared marriage, their roles become typified. Rachel is wife, lover, the one desired. Leah is the mother, the nurturing, fertile one. Each wants to have what the other has, to be what the other is.

Rachel has her husband's love, but wants his children, "Give me children, or I shall die!" (Gen 30:1). Like Sarah before her, she uses her maid servant to acquire offspring, but it does not bring her satisfaction. Leah has an abundance of children, mainly sons, which gives her a place of prominence. But what she desires is her husband's love, and she vainly hopes that each birth will secure that: "this time my husband will be joined to me, because I have borne him three sons" (Gen 29:34) and "now my husband will honor me, because I have borne him six sons" (Gen 30:20). The plight of each sister is seen in the "mandrake episode" (Gen 30:14–17) in which the sisters symbolically exchange their roles. Rachel bargains for mandrakes, a fertility drug, by granting Leah a night with Jacob.

How are we like Rachel or Leah? What complementarities or roles war within us? What or who are the modern equivalents of Laban that cast us in various roles? Must we choose between one role and the other?

REFLECTION QUESTIONS

Scripture readings: Genesis 29—31

- What questions come to mind as you read Leah's story? Make a note of them to bring to our next gathering.
- "Leah's eyes were lovely, and Rachel was graceful and beautiful" (Gen 29:17). Compare other translations for wording. What was being said about the importance of physical appearance? How does that compare to today's values?
- With whom do you identify, Rachel or Leah? Why? What about Bilhah and Zilpah? After exploring Hagar's story, do you see these two handmaids differently?
- Leah's first four sons are named, in succession: Reuben ("God sees her affliction"), Simeon ("God hears"), Levi ("Jacob will be joined to her"), and Judah ("I will praise the LORD"). What does the shift in emphasis with Judah's name say about Leah?
- Conversely, Rachel pleads to Jacob, "Give me sons, or I shall die." What does this say about Rachel's attitude?
- What does the story of the mandrakes tell you about the two women and their relationship to each other and to Jacob? In a world of patriarchy where women were without the rights we expect today, where did they have power and how did they exercise their influence?
- When Jacob decides to leave Laban, Rachel and Leah are in agreement with him and with each other. What does this say about their relationship to each other as sisters and their relationship to their father Laban?

CHALLENGE

Each of these two sisters has heartbreak in her life: Rachel is barren and Leah is unloved. Rather than support each other in their brokenness, both of them compete openly for their particular needs, chronicled in the names of their sons. What do you think is at the root of their competition? How might their circumstances have been handled differently? Can you think of another person, particularly a woman, with whom you find yourself competing? What does she have that you do not? What is at the root of your feeling? What escalates the competition between you? Can you think of a way to change from competition to coexistence? From coexistence to cooperation?

Space for your own reflections

LEAH'S PRAYER

Now Laban had two daughters; the name of the elder was Leah, and the name of the younger was Rachel. Leah's eyes were lovely, and Rachel was graceful and beautiful. Jacob loved Rachel; so he said, "I will serve you seven years for your younger daughter Rachel." (Gen 29:16–18)

When the LORD saw that Leah was unloved, he opened her womb; but Rachel was barren. Leah conceived and bore a son, and she named him Reuben; for she said, "Because the LORD has looked on my affliction; surely now my husband will love me." She conceived again and bore a son, and said, "Because the LORD has heard that I am hated, he has given me this son also"; and she named him Simeon. Again she conceived and bore a son, and said, "Now this time my husband will be joined to me, because I have borne him three sons"; therefore he was named Levi. She conceived again and bore a son, and said, "This time I will praise the LORD"; therefore she named him Judah; then she ceased bearing. (Gen 29:31–35)

Like Leah, we walk onto the stage of life judged first by our physical appearance. Like Leah, we allow that judgment to call forth jealousy and competition. What in our lives will prompt us to recall that God's love is unconditional; what will move us to "give glory to God"?

Judge us not,
O God of Leah,
for we are constantly being judged,
and judging ourselves by what others see when they look at us.
We know that we are formed in your image
and that we are perfect in your sight,
but often we are not content to look at ourselves through your eyes.
The world tells us our worth depends on our appearance and
sometimes we believe it.
Worse yet, we judge other women as well.
We foolishly seek to find our happiness

in places other than your tender heart.
Wash away our judgment and our jealousy;
place, in its stead, the abiding peace of knowing we are loved
and perfect in your sight.
Amen.

A CLOSER LOOK AT THE TEXT

With Leah we finish the story of the matriarchs. The rest of Genesis tells the story of Jacob's twelve sons, most especially Rachel's firstborn, Joseph. This will finish the story of the patriarchs, the receivers and keepers of the covenant. The next book of the Bible, Exodus, will open, in fact, with the genealogy of Jacob's sons and their prospering in Egypt. Then their fortunes change when "a new king arose over Egypt, who did not know Joseph" (Exod 1:8), and the stage is set for the story of the Exodus.

In our study we only looked at the second half of Genesis (chapters 12 to 50), the story of the patriarchs—or, in our case, the matriarchs. Let's take a look at how this portion fits into the larger context of the Bible.

The first five books of the Bible are referred to as the Pentateuch or, to Jews, the Torah, and they are Genesis, Exodus, Leviticus, Numbers, and Deuteronomy. Together they comprise the heart of the Hebrew scriptures because they tell the story of the covenant. Set within the universal context starting at creation, the Pentateuch tells the story of God's selecting a certain people and entering into relationship, a covenant, with them and all that entails. As they agree to take on the responsibilities to worship and obey only this God, they are formed into a distinct nation, united by faith more than by blood.

Lawrence Boadt provides this synopsis of the Torah in his book *Reading the Old Testament:*

> Genesis opens with the "history" of creation and the earliest human societies told in mythological forms. It rapidly narrows its aim to God's choice of the patriarchs Abraham, Isaac, Jacob and Joseph who receive his promise, carry out his plans, and prepare for his great act of deliverance from Egypt and the giving of his covenant at Mount Sinai.

Exodus tells the story of how God chose Moses to deliver Israel from slavery in Egypt and lead them to accept a covenant so that he would be their God and they would be his people (Ex 6:7). The book closes with detailed descriptions for the building of the tent of meeting and the ark of the covenant, central signs of God's presence with Israel.

Leviticus contains the laws and commandments that God gave to his newly sanctified people to obey as their share in the covenant relationship. These regulations deal mostly with sacrifice, feasts, priesthood, and the ritual obligations of worthiness and holiness.

Numbers adds many more laws and regulations about the twelve tribes and their organization as a holy people on the march. Chapters 10–20 then continue the story of Israel's wanderings in the desert, complete with a forty-year punishment for constantly rebelling against God and Moses.

Deuteronomy (or "second law" in Greek) is a later book composed entirely as a reflective speech of Moses which sums up the meaning of the exodus event and the desert journey, and reaffirms the importance of the covenant law as a guide for Israel's life in the promised land. It is Moses' "farewell speech" and supposedly takes place just as the people are ready to invade the promised land. (pp. 89–91)

The present structure of these five books has a definite shape. At the center stands the giving of the law on Mount Sinai in all its detail:

Genesis 1—11: Human Origins
    Divine blessing, sin, punishment, and mercy
Genesis 12—50: The Patriarchs
    Divine election, promise of progeny, land, and greatness
Exodus 1—18: God Saves His People
    The Exodus, God saves Israel and begins the fulfillment of the promise of land.
Exodus 19—24: The Book of Leviticus; Numbers 1—10: God's People Receive the Law
    The covenant embodied in the law binds Yahweh and Israel together forever and establishes a way of life.

Numbers 11—36: Journey to the Promised Land
    God leads the people to the Promised Land but punishes rebellion.
The Book of Deuteronomy: Final Words of Moses
    Moses' final warnings to obey the covenant or lose the land

The rest of the Old Testament can be divided into three categories: the Historical Books, the Wisdom Books, and the Prophetical Books. They are grouped accordingly and come in that order. You may want to take a look at the listing of the books in the table of contents in your own Bible to see how closely it corresponds to this breakdown.

Our next pair of women will come from the historical section, the Book of Ruth. After that, we move on to some women of the New Testament. It is important to see the larger context of these stories and to realize that we are only sampling the scriptures.

RUTH

Background

The timeline on p. 58 gives an overall picture of the history of Israel as it is recounted in scripture. The story of Ruth and Naomi is set in the time frame of the period of Judges. This post-Exodus era lasted about two hundred years from when the descendants of Abraham returned to and eventually occupied the Promised Land until the time when they had their first king, Saul.

"In the days when the judges ruled..." Thus begins the Book of Ruth. In this time before the orderly structure of the monarchy, life for the Israelites was basically one of political chaos, famine, and warfare. The "judges" referred to in the Bible were not elected or appointed in any planned way. Each one was a character who was raised up for his or her gifts during a time of emergency—usually to lead the Israelites against a threatening enemy. Between such battles, the judges retired from military leadership and the "normal" pattern of chaos returned. Without any infrastructure, periods of famine hit hard and often and people were on their own to find a way to survive. In some ways, the times resembled the American Wild West before law and order arrived. As it says in Judges 21:25, "all the people did what was right in their own eyes." It is in this setting that the story of these two women is told. Their challenge and eventual triumph are all the more remarkable for the hard times in which they find themselves.

Though these were chaotic times, they were not without standards in place. In addition to the Mosaic Law as received on Mount Sinai during the Exodus, the Israelite community during the period of judges had a primitive code that governed their actions. We see this evidenced in the custom of gleaning—allowing the poor, the widowed, and the stranger to follow the harvesters. Care and regard for the poor, widow, and stranger were imperative from the earliest stages of Judaism. Levirate law, which allowed a widow the right to children by mating with her deceased husband's brother, is also referred to in the Book of Ruth, although its application to Ruth, as a Moabite, is, to say the least, exceptional. Naomi is aware of the laws of the land and has Ruth use them to gain security. We even see a curious remnant of prevailing custom in 4:7 where the taking off one sandal and giving it to another sealed the contract between the two. This also verifies that the story was recorded after the fact in its phrasing, "Now this was the custom in former times in Israel..."

We have no information about the author of the Book of Ruth. Some scholars have suggested that it was originally a story told by women for other women. We have no way to verify the authorship. But this is a remarkable book in that the Bible is overwhelmingly about men, told from the point of view of men. Most of the time women are mentioned only as they relate to the men in the story. This situation is completely reversed in the Book of Ruth. The main characters are women and the main theme is their relationship with one another. The men are mentioned only because of their relationship to the two women. As often as the theme of journey shows up in scripture, it is the journey of men—Abraham, Jacob, Joseph, and so forth. Here the journey is that of two women. Enjoy.

Old Testament Timeline		
AGE OF THE PATRIARCHS	1900 BC	Abraham—Sarah & Hagar Isaac—Rebecca Jacob—Rachel & Leah Joseph
EXODUS EXPERIENCE	c. 1300 BC	Moses/Exodus/ Sinai covenant
PERIOD OF JUDGES	1250 BC	Invasion and settling of Canaan
MONARCHY Yahwist (Y)	1020 BC	Saul, David, Solomon

Elohist (E)	922 BC	Divided kingdom:
		  Northern—Israel
		  Southern—Judah
		
		Prophets: Amos (N), Hosea (N),
		Isaiah I (S), Micah (S)
		Continued

Continued		Syria conquers northern kingdom—Israel
	721 BC	
Deuteronomist (D)		Prophets: Jeremiah, Zephaniah, Nahum, Habakkuk
EXILE Priestly (P)	587 BC	Babylon conquers Judah Jerusalem destroyed Leaders deported to Babylon Prophets: Ezekiel, Isaiah II, Baruch
POST-EXILE JEDP	539 BC	Cyrus of Persia returns Jews to Israel Prophets: Haggai, Zechariah, Ezra, Nehemiah, Isaiah III, Obadiah, Malachi, Joel Alexander the Great conquers Israel Israel ruled by Ptolemies (Greeks in Egypt), then by Seleucids (Greeks in Syria)
	332 BC	Wisdom literature: Proverbs, Job, Ecclesiastes, Song of Songs, Wisdom
	167 BC	Maccabees revolt Daniel written
	63 BC	Romans conquer Israel
	AD 4	Birth of Christ

REFLECTION QUESTIONS

Scripture readings: Book of Ruth

- What questions come to mind as you read Ruth's story? Make a note of them to bring to our next gathering.
- What do you think Ruth's motives were for making a choice different from Orpah's? Did she have less to go back to? What forged her ties of affection to Naomi? Was she also choosing Yahweh over the gods of the Moabites? What stirred within her? Can you think of a similar, pivotal time in your life? What stirred within you and prompted you to make the decisions you did?
- Ruth's physical appearance is never referred to (recall that both Sarah and Rebecca were so beautiful they could be coveted by kings, Rachel was "graceful and beautiful" and Leah's "eyes were lovely"). Instead we see other attributes: *hesed*—(Hebrew for loving-kindness and faithfulness in her interactions with Naomi) and competence (each ephah of grain = 29 lbs.; the average man picked 2 lbs. a day). What appeals most to you about the person of Ruth?
- Regarding the threshing floor story (Ruth 3:1–18), what do you think is the importance here?
- What do you think of the character of Boaz? How would you assess the relationship between him and Ruth captured in the short exchange: Ruth: Why do you favor me? Boaz: Because I recognize the good you do (Ruth 2:10–11).

CHALLENGE

"Where you go, I will go; where you lodge, I will lodge; your people shall be my people, and your God my God. Where you die, I will die—there will I be buried" (Ruth 1:16b–17a). Ruth's *hesed* to Naomi was also *hesed* to all that represented. She proclaims unlimited compassion for another and takes on the other's lot in life. Read Mary's *Magnificat* (Luke 1:46–56), said to proclaim Mary's solidarity with the poor. What in your life calls forth this compassion, this *hesed*?

RUTH'S PRAYER

But Ruth said, "Do not press me to leave you or to turn back from following you! Where you go, I will go; where you lodge, I will lodge; your people shall be my people, and your God my God. Where you die, I will die—there will I be buried. May the LORD do thus and so to me, and more as well, if even death parts me from you!" (Ruth 1:16–17)

Ruth, the Moabite, teaches Israel what true faithfulness and love is and can be. She and Naomi are an example of a cooperative venture of women helping each other, generations helping each other. Together Ruth and Naomi conspire together for a future of hope. Ruth hands her life over to God and lives out her promise with exemplary faithfulness. She is the first person in scripture to show a preferential option for the poor and a model for true intimacy, an image of God's unfailing love.

Show us your loving-kindness,
O God of Ruth.
May we recognize your compassionate heart
and, emboldened by your love for us,
extend that kind of love to others:
to those closest to us who share our lives—
may we be constant and kind in our care for them;
to those with whom we share our human struggles—
may we uplift and sustain them by our solidarity and support.
We thank you for the example of others who have loved heroically and
    compassionately
and we ask you to bless them for their goodness.
Amen.

A CLOSER LOOK AT THE TEXT

All of the stories that we have looked at from Genesis were about the transmission and centrality of the covenant. We have here a simple story that seems to exist outside of that purpose but, in reality, is the perfect example to Israel of what covenant love looks like. This independent gem of a story puts flesh on covenant love, showing Israel the faithfulness and devotion that the covenant is all about.

The picture painted of Ruth is one of selfless love and prefigures another woman at the start of the Christian scriptures who acts in the same way, Mary of Nazareth. Ruth promises, "Where you go, I will go; where you lodge, I will lodge; your people shall be my people, and your God my God. Where you die, I will die— there will I be buried" (Ruth 1:16b–17a). This is complete surrender of self to another. Like Mary's *fiat,* it is unconditional and irrevocable even as it is completely without assurances about the future. Both Ruth and Mary live out their commitment with remarkable faithfulness.

In the choices they make, both Ruth and Mary give over their lives to God and throw their lot in with the poor and disenfranchised. Mary's *Magnificat* sings of her lowliness and her obedience and promises to raise up the lowly and bring hope to the poor. Ruth takes on that same lot in uniting herself to Naomi, a widow. Widows were the most marginalized of all Israel's citizens. Without husbands or sons to advocate and provide for them, they were without any means of support. In uniting herself to Naomi, Ruth takes that future on for herself even though she had the option of staying in Moab and remarrying. In Ruth's relationship to the older woman, Naomi, we also see overtones of the story of Mary and Elizabeth which we will discuss when we come to Elizabeth's story.

There is a parallel as well between Boaz and Joseph, two just men who transgress the letter of the law to take into their protection women who would, very likely, not have survived without them. Though both are secondary characters, their saving action is pivotal to the story and assures the outcome. They are both willing to take on the role of father to a son that is not theirs. For Boaz, he is the natural father but the child is not his heir. For Joseph, he is not the natural father but takes on all the responsibilities of that role.

There is also, of course, the same setting for both stories—Bethlehem, the house of bread. At the return of Naomi with Ruth and at the birth of Obed, the small city is abuzz with excitement. Centuries later it will hum with excitement again when three visitors appear from the East seeking another newborn child.

Scripture tells us that Obed will become the father of Jesse, the father of David, from whose line the Christ will come. Thus, the Moabite woman becomes the great-grandmother of Israel's greatest king and part of the lineage of Jesus.

NAOMI

Background

Though the title is the Book of Ruth, Naomi is the main character in this story. She is the protagonist who initiates the action and makes decisions. The story begins and ends with her in Bethlehem.

Because there were no government structures in place during the time of the judges, when famine struck there was no help available, not even a king to whom one could appeal. Thus it fell to Elimelech, the husband of Naomi, to make a difficult choice. Just as Jacob left the Promised Land in a time of famine, so Elimelech, Naomi, and their two sons left Bethlehem of Judah for the plateau of Moab where they hoped economic conditions would be better. It was not an easy thing to leave the land God had promised to Abraham. This was not only the land of their ancestors, the patriarchs, it was also the land for which they endured forty years in the desert and for which they then fought to regain.

The plight of the family was not unlike that of immigrants anywhere. Forced to leave what they knew and loved, they were in a strange land and the hoped-for good fortune did not occur. Some time after their arrival, Elimelech died. In the ensuing ten years, Naomi watched her sons take Moabite wives, Orpah and Ruth, but then both the sons died without having had children. Naomi was left without husband, sons, or heirs. The dying out of the family line was the greatest of evils to befall Naomi. The value and role of a woman was to produce children and ensure the continuation of the family line. It was of such importance that there was a law to provide for such cases, the levirate law based on Deuteronomy 25:5–10. The levirate law required that when a man died without having had children, his widow should marry his brother, and their son should receive the name and inheritance of the deceased brother. Because Naomi had no sons and was too old to bear more, the levirate law did not seem to offer hope in this case. There was no way to continue the family line.

Naomi was now a widow. *Va-tisher,* the Hebrew word that describes her, means "and she was left." The term aptly described Naomi's condition. She was alone and without any means to raise up heirs or to care for herself. Her only remaining connection was her two Moabite daughters-in-law, Orpah and Ruth, themselves widows but widows still within the childbearing years.

Naomi shows strength of character, however, in her ability to move on in the midst of loss. Leaving the Promised Land was her husband's decision but returning was hers. She hears that food is available there once again and resolves to return.

Because Orpah and Ruth are young enough, they would normally return home to their parents so that another marriage could be arranged for them. Something inspired them instead to set out with Naomi on the four- to five-day journey across the Jordan River and desert of Judah. Not only are they leaving what they know and taking on a perilous journey, they are entering "enemy" territory. The Moabites are the only people in scripture that the Torah condemns (Deut 23:2–6). There is little chance in Israel that they would be welcomed and almost none that they would have the opportunity to marry again.

Naomi knows what awaits the young women and clearly wants the best for them. The scene where they divide is particularly touching. She tries to send them back home with encouragement to have a husband and home. She kisses them goodbye and cries with loud sobs. Both of them protest they will not leave her, for the bond of affection is obviously mutual. Naomi urges them further and, finally, Orpah kisses her and leaves in tears. Her decision, though painful, is a sensible and good one. All the more remarkable, then, is Ruth's decision to stay. Her words show the depth of her commitment to Naomi: "Do not press me to leave you or to turn back from following you! Where you go, I will go; where you lodge, I will lodge; your people shall be my people, and your God my God" (Ruth 1:16).

Once Naomi returns to Bethlehem, she again shows her concern for Ruth and her gentle wisdom in guiding her in actions that secure a future. In the end, the focus returns to Naomi when the newborn son of Ruth and Boaz is placed upon Naomi's lap.

REFLECTION QUESTIONS

Scripture readings: Book of Ruth

- What questions come to mind as you read Naomi's story? Make a note of them to bring to our next gathering.
- Do you know of any families like Naomi's that are forced by poverty to move to a foreign land, and then marry natives of that land? What difficulties would you expect in such marriages?
- After the loss of her husband and sons, Naomi went back to Bethlehem. It could no longer offer her the sanctuary of family. But she made the decision, in her grief, to move on. Can you recall a time of loss (e.g., marriage ending, no means of support, nothing to define who you are), when you seemed no longer to be what you were before (you were a *vatisher,* a leftover or husk)? How did you respond?
- Naomi made a special effort to see that Orpah and Ruth felt free to follow their own star rather than be tied down by obligation to care for her in her old age. Do you know an old person who has done the same? Or the opposite?
- Israelite society provided for the poor by allowing them to glean grain after the harvesters. How does our society provide for the poor? Do you think we provide adequately?
- The women of Bethlehem credit Ruth with Naomi's happiness, the women name the baby, and Ruth delivers the child to the arms of Naomi. How does this passage speak to you?

CHALLENGE

Though Naomi is widowed and childless, she acts in a way that brings hope to the future. She brings her wisdom to bear in advising Ruth, ensuring both her future and, eventually, her grandson's. What better world do you wish for the next generation? Can you imagine ways to help bring that about?

NAOMI'S PRAYER

Naomi her mother-in-law said to her, "My daughter, I need to seek some security for you, so that it may be well with you." (Ruth 3:1)

Then the women said to Naomi, "Blessed be the LORD, who has not left you this day without next-of-kin; and may his name be renowned in Israel! He shall be to you a restorer of life and a nourisher of your old age; for your daughter-in-law who loves you, who is more to you than seven sons, has borne him." Then Naomi took the child and laid him in her bosom, and became his nurse. The women of the neighborhood gave him a name, saying, "A son has been born to Naomi." They named him Obed; he became the father of Jesse, the father of David. (Ruth 4:14–17)

Naomi acts in ways that not only provide security for Ruth, but also bring her happiness. She is a model of *hesed,* the loving-kindness of God. Together Naomi and Ruth are an example of the love at the heart of the covenant.

Empower us,
O God of Naomi,
to rise from the bone-jarring losses of life
to follow your lead with our hearts, hands, and feet
and become what you call us to be.
Give us the courage to see and to name those ways
in which our world denies us our birthright as children of God.
Help us to use the experience and wisdom of our years
to think creatively and act boldly in counteracting injustice.
May our gift to the next generation be a better world,
a world that will receive their gifts with joy.
Amen.

A CLOSER LOOK AT THE TEXT

It is easy to characterize the Book of Ruth as an engaging story of two women banding together against great odds to triumph through love, loyalty, and faith over adversity—and that would be correct. But it is also possible to look beneath the surface for some of the other themes that are more challenging, particularly to the readers for which it was written.

The first issue worthy of a closer look is Ruth's ethnic identity as a Moabite. The Moabites are not just foreigners, they are one of Israel's most hated enemies. Back during the time when Israel was wandering through the wilderness, the women of Moab tried to corrupt the Israelite men. As such, Moabite women are specifically excluded in Deuteronomy 23:2–6 from ever being a part of the Israelite community. Depending on when the Book of Ruth was actually written, a Moabite heroine would have been particularly scandalous. Although the story itself is placed in the period of the judges, writing it down or choosing to include it in the Hebrew Canon came much later. If it is dated from a time before the Exile, it can be a simple story with a moral. If, however, it is dated from a time at or after the Exile when Israel is struggling to assert its national identity, the story becomes a parable on a par with Jesus' story of the Good Samaritan.

Compounding the choice of a Moabite as the heroine is the fact that the law of levirate is applied to her. This law allowed an Israelite widow without heirs to mate with her deceased husband's brother to produce an heir. In this way, Israelite families and property were protected. Here, however, the levirate law is applied to Moabite daughter-in-law of an Israelite widow—a stretch of both the letter and the intent of the law.

Boaz interprets the levirate law in a way that favors the widow and ensures the other kinsmen would bow out of the agreement. By framing it as he does, a marriage with Ruth could mean that the land in question might ultimately revert to an heir of Naomi's—a condition that Boaz is willing to agree to but that the other man is not. Boaz then agrees to both redeem the land and marry Ruth and allows the kinsmen a gracious way out at the same time that he appears beneficent and just.

In so doing, Boaz models an interpretation of the law that rises above the literal. Just as Ruth is a challenging example to Israel of *hesed* being displayed by a foreigner, Boaz challenges Israel to a higher justice than a narrow rendering of the law. It stands in opposition to any narrow reading of the law that would be used to oppress another and points, instead, to a higher criterion, justice.

ELIZABETH

Background

With Elizabeth we make the transition to the New Testament or Christian scriptures. It is important to remember, however, that Elizabeth is a Jewish woman in a Jewish culture—as are Mary and all the women in the remaining scripture, except the Samaritan woman. Judaism and the Hebrew scriptures have special meaning for us as Christians. Here is the cradle into which Jesus was born and from which Christianity will derive. We fail to appreciate the richness and uniqueness of the Hebrew scriptures, however, if we only look at them as precursor to the Christian scriptures. As Lawrence Boadt says in *Reading the Old Testament*:

> In some ways Christians are guilty of seeing too much connection between the Old and New Testaments. By seeing the Old Testament as primarily foreshadowing and preparing for Christ, mainly through prediction, they have often left little room for appreciating Israel's experiences of divine action as part of their own search to know God....
>
> Christians, faithful to their beliefs, must proclaim that Christ is the center and fulfillment of the Old Testament message and the highest expression of God's self-revelation for those who have the faith to see it; but they must not believe that God has rejected what he had earlier revealed, or withdrawn his covenant with Israel. In God's designs there is a mysterious purpose why he does not choose to have the whole world know Christ....It is our proper stance today to respect Jewish faith as it makes the revelation of the Old Testament alive in the twentieth century. We need to learn all that the word "covenant" implies before we can speak of a "new" covenant. If Christ is proclaimed as the fullness of Israel's faith, then God help us if there is no Israel to show us what that means.
>
> The Old Testament is a great treasure chest in which a wealth of truth about God lies waiting for us to discover it. No Christian can

fully understand the New Testament revelation of God if he or she has not seen a glimpse of that wealth. It is wonderfully expressed by the saying of Jesus, who asked his disciples if they understood his teaching about the Kingdom of God. When they answered "yes," he summed up the ideal disciple in the words, "Every scribe who has been trained for the Kingdom of heaven is like a homeowner who brings out of his storeroom both the new and the old" (Mt 13:52). (pp. 540–41)

To fully appreciate these women that we are studying, we need to recognize them as being Jews, just as Jesus was. The first Christians were Jews and it is impossible to understand Christianity without looking first at Judaism. Scholars recognize now that the two religions did not abruptly part with the fall of the temple in AD 70, though that was a hastening factor. Rather, throughout the first three centuries, they differentiated and began to take on distinct shape. When looking at the past, Christians have often been guilty of *supersessionism,* or holding that Christianity supersedes Judaism. We have ignored any contribution that the Old Testament or that Judaism made in their own right, aside from laying a groundwork for our own belief system. We have, further, failed to recognize that Judaism and the Hebrew scriptures still have something to say to us today. Instead Christianity has often disparaged them as useless or, worse yet, evil—with disastrous results, including anti-Semitism.

REFLECTION QUESTIONS

Scripture readings: Luke 1

- What questions come to mind as you read Elizabeth's story? Make a note of them to bring to our next gathering.
- What does Elizabeth's conceiving in her old age say to you now that you have read the stories of the matriarchs?
- What does Elizabeth's conceiving in her old age say to you about how God brings about the impossible? "And now, your relative Elizabeth in her old age has also conceived a son; and this is the sixth month for her who was said to be barren. For nothing will be impossible with God" (Luke 1:36–37).
- The words of the Hail Mary are Elizabeth's gift to us. How has that prayer been a part of your life? The second joyful mystery of the rosary is the Visitation. How has praying on this mystery been important to you?
- When have you, like Elizabeth, intuited something, or had the Spirit "leap" within you?
- Who in your life has been the kind of friend that Elizabeth was to Mary? Who knows more about you? Who recognized the good? Who supported you in your deepest need?
- Elizabeth said, "And why has this happened to me, that the mother of my Lord comes to me?" (Luke 1:43). When in your life have you been most astounded that God has shown you favor?

CHALLENGE

If you have not already done so with our other women studied, use this familiar story of Elizabeth to write a midrash or a poem, or create some other representation of this story.

ELIZABETH'S PRAYER

In those days Mary set out and went with haste to a Judean town in the hill country, where she entered the house of Zechariah and greeted Elizabeth. When Elizabeth heard Mary's greeting, the child leaped in her womb. And Elizabeth was filled with the Holy Spirit and exclaimed with a loud cry, "Blessed are you among women, and blessed is the fruit of your womb. And why has this happened to me, that the mother of my Lord comes to me? For as soon as I heard the sound of your greeting, the child in my womb leaped for joy. And blessed is she who believed that there would be a fulfillment of what was spoken to her by the Lord." (Luke 1:39–45)

These words from Elizabeth are the first confession of faith in Christ in all of Luke's Gospel. When Elizabeth greets Mary as "blessed among women," she is echoing the phrase used of two brave Old Testament women who destroyed the power of enemy leaders by assassinating them—Jael (Judg 5:24) and Judith (Jdt 13:18). This prepares the way for Mary's *Magnificat,* which praises God for over-throwing those in power. There is, however, an important contrast. Whereas Judith and Jael killed Israel's enemies by their own hand, in Mary, God "has done great things" and "brought down the powerful," simply because Mary had believed what was spoken to her (Margaret Hebblethwaite, *Six New Gospels,* pp. 10, 11).

Visit us,
O God of Elizabeth.
May our spirits quicken at your coming,
the doors of our homes and hearts be swift
to swing open and embrace you.
May we recognize you in whatever form your coming takes,
in the needy friend, the stranger, the child, the unexpected interruption.
May we learn to trust you with our deepest longings and heartfelt dreams,
to remember how you kept your promises to Elizabeth and Mary
and to trust that you will remember us as well,
for nothing is impossible for you.
Amen.

A CLOSER LOOK AT THE TEXT

Identifying the "authors" J, E, D, and P of the Old Testament required quite a bit of detective work. As we come to the New Testament, however, specifically to the Gospels, our authors are named—Matthew, Mark, Luke, and John. It behooves us at the outset, however, to take a look at the overall context of the Gospels and some of the unique characteristics of each of these four "familiar" writers.

Matthew, Mark, and Luke are referred to as the *Synoptic Gospels,* which literally means "seen together." They parallel one another and have much in common. Mark was the first Gospel written, about AD 65. Both Matthew and Luke draw from Mark and from another common, outside, but undiscovered source that scripture scholars call "Q" or *quelle,* which is German for the word "source." Both Matthew and Luke wrote about AD 85. Each wrote to a different audience for a specific purpose that helped determine the choices made in what to include and how to say it.

John shares much less with the other three and has a large amount of material unique to that Gospel. It is written significantly later, about AD 100, and is markedly different in style as well as in purpose.

Though the Synoptics are generally in sync with one another, they vary considerably when it comes to the infancy narratives. Mark does not have an infancy narrative. Instead he begins rather abruptly with John the Baptist appearing in the desert, quoting Isaiah, "Prepare the way of the Lord" (Mark 1:3). (This gives us one clue to the importance and centrality of John the Baptist, Elizabeth's son.) Matthew begins with the genealogy of Jesus and tells the story of his birth with details completely different from those in Luke's Gospel. Matthew tells of Joseph's dreams, of the Magi, of the flight into Egypt, and of the killing of Bethlehem's children. Luke, on the other hand, devotes two full chapters to his infancy narrative. Like Mark he begins with John the Baptist but with the announcement of his birth—the angel appearing to Zechariah. Luke sets up two parallel stories, John's and Jesus'. Both have an annunciation, a miracle pregnancy, and a canticle. Then Luke goes on to the birth and offers details not given elsewhere: the census and birth in a stable, the angels and the shepherds, and, later, the presentation in the temple with the reaction of both Simeon and Anna.

John's Gospel begins, not with an infancy narrative but with a christological hymn, "In the beginning was the Word…" This sets a tone and style that will continue throughout John's writing.

As we read each of these evangelists we will see how they bring to the text their own outlook, context, purpose, and audience.

Just as John the Baptist takes center stage at the outset of two of the four Gospels, so does his mother Elizabeth in the context of this study. She stands in the footsteps of the women who have gone before her. Like Sarah she conceives in her old age. As with Hagar and Rebecca, the birth is announced ahead of time. Like Rachel she longs for a child and is, at last, rewarded. She acts with the wisdom and compassion of Naomi for Ruth in her understanding and embrace of Mary.

As her son will be a prophet, so, too, is Elizabeth. Unlike her husband, she shows no sign of hesitation at the divinely appointed role of bringing this child into the world, and when Mary shows up at her doorstep, Elizabeth greets her as the "mother of my Lord." Thus, filled with the Holy Spirit, she makes a prophetic statement. She recognizes that Mary is favored or blessed because she bears the Lord: "Blessed are you among women, and blessed is the fruit of your womb" (Luke 1:42). She also recognizes that Mary is blessed because of her faith: "Blessed is she who believed that there would be a fulfillment of what was spoken to her by the Lord" (Luke 1:45).

MARY OF NAZARETH

Background

We add the clarifying description "of Nazareth" for Mary because we will soon look at other Marys: Mary of Bethany and Mary Magdalene. Yet this Mary, Mary of Nazareth, is without need of introduction. Indeed, the challenge becomes to look at her with fresh eyes because, as Catholic women, we have known her all our lives.

As we seek to see her with fresh eyes, it is helpful to consider what ideas about Mary we already bring with us. This will not only allow us to be enriched by one another's point of view, but it will also help us choose to see Mary and her role in God's plan in, perhaps, new and previously unseen ways.

One of the basic stances we might take toward God is whether we see God as transcendent or immanent. God is, of course, both, but if we tend to see God as transcendent, that means we identify with God as holy, divine, separate, and powerful. If we tend to see God as immanent, we identify with God as loving, accessible, and involved in human affairs. In Old Testament terms we see how such distinctions and different senses of God advised the images used by different authors or strains in scripture. Thus, although it is a bit of an oversimplification, it can still be accurately stated that the Priestly writer of the Old Testament had a transcendent sense of God. Consider the God of Creation in Genesis 1 who moved over the waters in power and mystery and had only to speak and there was light. The Yahwist writer, on the other hand, had a more immanent sense of God and used images in the Genesis 2 creation story of God molding clay, breathing life into it, and walking in the cool of the evening. One might say that the transcendent is a kind of vertical line with God above and that the immanent corresponds to a horizontal line with God alongside. God is both, of course, and is, perhaps, best found where the two dimensions intersect—thus the value of knowing our own preference and enriching our understanding with other images.

Similarly, our stance toward Mary is often determined by whether we emphasize the holiness she shares with God or the humanity she shares with us. For, like her son Jesus, she exists in both worlds. Consider one of her most basic titles, that of Virgin Mother. Virgin implies attributes of separateness, being set aside or saved for a special purpose, not like most women. It emphasizes Mary's purity and goodness and her unique role. Mother, on the other hand, underscores the foundational attribute that all women and, indeed, all humanity share, for all are born of mothers and most women become mothers themselves. Thus Mary as mother makes her accessible to us all. Within the title Virgin Mother, therefore, both dimensions exist.

In her relationship with Elizabeth as depicted in their meeting, Mary exemplifies both dimensions, for Elizabeth greets her as "mother of my Lord" but also praises her as a woman of faith, "blessed is she who believed." They share the human dimension of their pregnancies in common as well as the knowledge that they are cooperating in a divine purpose. Part of why Mary comes to Elizabeth is that she may well be the only other person who could accept or understand Mary's situation.

REFLECTION QUESTIONS

Scripture readings: Luke 1

- What questions come to mind as you read Mary's story? Make a note of them to bring to our next gathering.
- Over the years artists have represented Mary in a variety of occupations and places at the time of the Annunciation. Where do you think she was, and what was she doing when the angel appeared to her?
- What similarities and differences do you see between the relationship of Mary and Elizabeth and those of other women we have studied?
- Which attributes of Mary most appeal to you—that she is holy like God or human like us? Why?
- Why do you think Mary has the universal appeal that she has had through the ages and across cultures?
- All of the joyful mysteries of the rosary feature Mary—the Annunciation, the Visitation, the Nativity, the Presentation, finding Jesus in the temple. Which do you find yourself most drawn to? Why? What images do you meditate upon?
- How would you explain to a non-Catholic the place of Mary in Catholic devotion? In your life?

- How would you respond to Catholics who use devotion to Mary as a "test" of one's "Catholicity"?

CHALLENGE

Write about a time when your prayers to Mary or reflection on her made an important difference in your life. What did you learn from that?

Space for your own reflections

MARY'S PRAYER

The angel said to her, "The Holy Spirit will come upon you, and the power of the Most High will overshadow you; therefore the child to be born will be holy; he will be called Son of God. And now, your relative Elizabeth in her old age has also conceived a son; and this is the sixth month for her who was said to be barren. For nothing will be impossible with God." Then Mary said, "Here am I, the servant of the Lord; let it be with me according to your word." Then the angel departed from her. (Luke 1:35–38)

Elizabeth was there and prompted both Zechariah and Mary to proclaim their canticles that are both preserved and prayed as part of the prayer of the Church and are great gifts to all generations. Here Mary echoes the words of Hannah in proclaiming God's goodness, but she does more as she announces a new age of justice. She stands solidly here with the God of the lowly.

Come upon us, O God of Mary,
that we might be Christ-bearers to a world in need
of your love, your light, your message of hope and reconciliation.
Aware of our lowliness at so bold a request,
we are encouraged that one among us, a woman like us,
had the courage to say yes and, so, made it possible
for all of us to share in the work of creating the world anew.
May all that we do proclaim your greatness.
May our spirit find joy in you as our savior.
May your Holy Spirit within us enable us
to give every good thing to those who are hungry—
for food, understanding, hope, love, or holiness.
May we raise up what is lowly by bestowing dignity on all whom we meet,
and by widening our circle of understanding and
gifting the next generation with the model of accepting all your people.
May we be encouraged by knowing that nothing we are asked to do in this life
has not already been done, and done well, by Mary.
Amen.

A CLOSER LOOK AT THE TEXT

The Magnificat

In the prayer life of the Church—the Liturgy of the Hours or Divine Office—the *Magnificat* is sung every day at Morning Prayer. Mary's song of joy is a song of great promise for what the coming redeemer will bring to all people, but most especially to the poor, the oppressed, and the marginalized. In her canticle, Mary draws upon the history of God's faithfulness and deliverance of Israel, revealing a familiarity with both the story and the psalms of the Jews. In this, she echoes Hannah's canticle in 1 Samuel 2:1–10.

Mary not only looks back, however, she also looks forward to the anticipated deliverance. She promises a transformed social order where the hungry are fed and the lowly are raised up while the rich are sent away hungry and the powerful are brought low. This reversal anticipates the resurrection in its radical impact. The gospel message of good news for the poor is introduced here in Mary's words. She speaks of a spiritual realm that is manifested in social, economical, and political reality. God's might, mercy, and holiness are available for those who suffer, for those with whom God has chosen to identify in becoming one of us. Our God is a God of history who acts in the here and now. Mary acts as a prophet of the poor, representing all those who have suffered, but whom God vindicates. The emphasis is not on her lowliness or insignificance as compared to God. Rather it is on God's mindfulness of her and all those like her. Mary's words and stance before God have given inspiration and hope to countless millions since she first sang this song.

The strength and prophetic nature of Mary's *Magnificat* strikes a startling picture of her. If we add to that her many other appearances outside of the infancy narratives—her role at Cana and her presence at the foot of the Cross and in the Upper Room—she emerges as a woman of great strength. However she may have been painted or typecast over the years as submissive or silent, if we look at her as she appears in the scriptures, she is most definitely neither. Here we see a woman who, like Elizabeth, imparts to her son much of her own indomitable character.

MARTHA OF BETHANY

Background

Above all, maintain constant love for one another, for love covers a multitude of sins. Be hospitable to one another without complaining. Like good stewards of the manifold grace of God, serve one another with whatever gift each of you has received. (1 Pet 4:8–10)

There is a saying in the Talmud, "Hospitality is a form of worship." Hospitality was, and remains, an extremely important value in the Middle East. In biblical times, without any infrastructure to provide for travelers, hospitality took on added significance. Often it afforded the only comfort and safety available. Perhaps the closest comparison for us would be the welcome one might rightfully expect from a homestead during the days of the westward migration.

For Martha, living as she did on the outskirts of Jerusalem, opening her home to others went beyond the customary taking in of travelers. Jerusalem attracted Jesus and his followers and also created the need for them to withdraw to a private place. It ensured that he and his followers would frequently come to the home she shared with her sister Mary and brother Lazarus.

Some of the daily tasks required by women to run a household in the time of Christ would include:

- Grinding grain for bread, then mixing, kneading, and baking the bread for the day.
- Purchasing meat at a market or preparing an animal from the household's flock for meat to eat, then cooking that meat.
- Obtaining fuel for the fire, building and tending the fire for cooking and for heat at night.
- Caring for any animals in the household.
- If there were servants in a household, overseeing the tasks they take on and providing for their needs in addition to the family's needs.

- Carding, spinning, and weaving threads of various kinds to make cloth for clothing, bedding, and other household uses.
- Sewing clothing for household members.
- Drawing the water for each day's requirements.
- Cleaning the house.
- Washing the utensils and dishes used in meal preparation and eating.
- Washing the family's clothing.
- Teaching and disciplining and loving the children in the household.

REFLECTION QUESTIONS

Scripture readings: Luke 10:38–42; John 11:1–44, 12:1–2

- What questions come to mind as you read Martha's story? Make a note of them to bring to our next meeting.
- In Luke's story of Martha and Mary, we see two sisters of different temperaments at odds with each other. How often have you heard this story developed along those lines? What do you think this story is about?
- When you heard this story in terms of the worker versus the listener, with whom did you identify? Why?
- What things in your life distract you and keep you from taking time for your spiritual growth?
- What do you make of Jesus' saying, "Mary has chosen the better part" (Luke 10:42)? What kind of judgment or issues come up around that?
- "Jesus loved Martha and her sister and Lazarus" (John 11:5). What kind of home do you think Martha had created? Why did Jesus love to come there? What elements of Martha's home have you created in your own?
- Martha's words with Jesus are the words of one who is honest and who knows him well. If you were honest with Jesus, more honest than you have ever been, what would you say to him?
- What questions do you think went through Martha's mind as she waited for Jesus to arrive? Grief-stricken, Martha greeted Jesus, "Lord, if you had been here, my brother would not have died" (John 11:21). Have you ever thought or felt the same way? How can faith help us deal with grief?

- Compare John 11:27 with Mark 8:29. What significance do you find in these similar words being spoken by Peter and by Martha?

CHALLENGE

Martha, the woman of action in Luke 10, becomes Martha, the woman proclaiming faith in John 11. How do you try to incorporate faith and action in your own life?

Space for your own reflections

MARTHA'S PRAYER

But Martha was distracted by her many tasks; so she came to him and asked, "Lord, do you not care that my sister has left me to do all the work by myself? Tell her then to help me." (Luke 10:40)

She said to him, "Yes, Lord, I believe that you are the Messiah, the Son of God, the one coming into the world." (John 11:27)

Martha first appears in Luke as a whirlwind of activity "worried and distracted by many things." She is admonished that "there is need of only one thing" (Luke 10:41–42a). Her long friendship with Jesus, her openness to what he teaches, and the tragic death of her brother changes all that. In John's Gospel, she is a woman who takes initiative, gets things done, deals with her loss and grief, and expresses deep faith in Jesus.

Welcome,
O God of Martha,
into our homes, our hearts, our lives.
Come join us at table, dine with us, laugh, drink, and talk with us.
Into the circle let us invite all who come with you—
no strangers here, only friends whom we have not yet met.
May every detail of our living be made sacred by your presence,
nothing too small or inconsequential to serve your purpose.
Into the busyness of our days, bring the satisfaction of knowing it is you
*   whom we serve,*
for you have made our labor holy.
May we, like Martha, live our lives in such a way as to invite others to
*   come to know you and,*
at the end of our days,
may we, like Martha, arrive at faith great enough
to proclaim our Savior and Lord.
Amen.

A CLOSER LOOK AT THE TEXT

Luke devotes four verses to Martha and her sister Mary. John, on the other hand, uses most of chapter 11 to tell the story of Martha, Mary, and the raising of their brother Lazarus, and gives over another ten verses of chapter 12 to another story set in their home. Yet, typically, it is the story from Luke that people most often associate with the name of Martha.

That association is not a particularly positive one. The plot of the story pits the two sisters one against the other, and Jesus says that Mary "has chosen the better part" (Luke 10:42b), thus relegating Martha to second place. Jesus chides Martha gently but does not heed her request, leaving her silenced. She is, hence, the loser, not the model with whom the reader is supposed to identify—but the one with whom some of us do.

Commentators have argued the case for centuries. In medieval times, the story was used as proof that religious life was superior to secular life—vestiges of that remain to this day. Even then, however, Teresa of Avila took exception to that understanding. In *The Interior Castle* she wrote to her sisters, who were a contemplative order, "Believe me, Martha and Mary must join together in order to show hospitality to the Lord and have Him always present and not host Him badly by failing to give Him something to eat. How would Mary, always seated at His feet, provide Him with food if her sister did not help her?" (VII, iv).

As we look at the four evangelists, one of the helpful biblical tools to use is to look at the audience to whom each was writing and to consider what purpose each Gospel was meant to serve. Both Luke and John write about Martha but make different choices about what to say. Some biblical scholars find clues to Luke's choices by looking at the community to whom he was writing. Writing in the eighth decade, Luke is especially concerned that fledgling Christianity be "politically correct." He takes pains to show that Christian men and women fit the standards of behavior for Roman society. In the first few decades of Christianity, the churches Paul founded and/or wrote to had many women in untraditional roles as prophets, deacons, teachers, apostles, and leaders of house churches. By the time Luke is writing, however, two things have happened: (1) they are into the second generation of Christians, no longer expecting the imminent return of Christ and thus looking to a more distant future, and (2) Christianity has become a suspect religion and has begun to be persecuted. Additionally, there was debate at this time over the roles of women and over emerging offices in house churches, some of which had been founded and led by women. So some scholars interpret Luke's story as addressing these issues to say that the "better portion" for women is to sit in silence and listen.

John, on the other hand, is writing significantly later than Luke for considerably different reasons. Luke is seeking, "after investigating everything carefully from the very first, to write an orderly account" (Luke 1:3). He is a storyteller deciding what to include and how to tell the story of Jesus as he determines what his readers, his community, want and need to know about Jesus. John's Gospel is less of a story and more of a theological reflection about the significance of Jesus' life. His themes drive the narrative. Every story is there to make a point about Jesus and to underscore the central truths of his incarnation, passion, death, and resurrection.

At any rate, it is ironic that Luke's Martha and Mary story often takes precedence over John's much larger story—a story with much more to say theologically. Luke's story offers an interesting portrait of human nature and addresses the importance of prayer but is not particularly profound theologically. Some have even challenged the construction that would pit prayer against actions. The two are so much of a tandem team in our Catholic tradition. The motto of the Benedictines sums it up in "Ora et labora"—pray and work. Aside from a point about prayer, Luke's story seems to deal with sibling rivalry between the two sisters. In so doing, he creates an either/or mentality that survives to our own time. For some women, it is frustrating that the smaller, less theologically significant vignette of Martha in Luke has become the popular image for her rather than the image presented in John's longer narrative.

In John's Gospel, a much different Martha emerges. There is no hint of tension between the sisters in John. Together they send word to Jesus and together they wait for him to come. They both speak the same words to him in greeting, "Lord, if you had been here, my brother would not have died" (John 11:21, 32). In John, everything that happens is significant for its foreshadowing of the passion. The resurrection of Lazarus prefigures Jesus' own resurrection. It was because of raising Lazarus that the Pharisees determined to kill Jesus. It is in preparation for his burial that Mary anoints Jesus and Martha's profession of faith is a capstone to the story.

The words of Martha in her profession of faith are remarkable. A close read reveals that she progresses through stages of faith in her dialogue with Jesus. First she calls him "Lord" and complains that if he had come sooner her brother would not have died. She still believes, however, that "even now, I know that God will give you whatever you ask of him" (John 11:22)—a stance reminiscent of Jesus' mother Mary's at Cana in John 2:1–12. Jesus then states the belief held by many rabbis of his time, "Your brother will rise again" (John 11:23). To this she agrees with the partial expression of faith, "I know he will rise again in the resurrection on the last day" (John 11:24). But then Jesus goes beyond conventional religious thought with the startling revelation, "I am the resurrection and the life. Those who believe in me, even though they die, will live; and everyone who lives and believes in me will never die" (John 11:25–26). Here Martha gives an extraordinarily mature christological profession of faith, saying, "I believe that you are the Messiah [i.e., the Christ], the Son of God, the one coming into the world" (John 11:27). Her words incorporate lines right out of John's prologue—Jesus is the Christ, the Son of God, who comes into the world from God. She expresses the same faith, in similar words, as Peter's in Matthew 16:16 for which he receives Jesus' blessing and the "keys to the kingdom." And she does all this before the miracle of Lazarus being raised from the dead. She then runs, as a true witness, to tell her sister that Jesus is with them. Martha, the noncontemplative, busy woman of action in Luke, becomes, in John, a prophet of the resurrection and witness to Jesus on a par with Peter's testimony of faith.

MARY OF BETHANY

Background

All four gospel accounts have a story of a woman anointing Jesus, which is testimony to its significance. It is impossible to determine the number of incidents represented. The Eastern churches have long believed in three distinctly different anointings: (1) the one at Simon's house as told in Mark and Matthew, (2) the one done by the sinner in Luke, and (3) the one by Mary of Bethany in John. What is clear, however, is that although there may have originally been only one anointing retold several ways (think of Sarah being passed off as Abraham's sister), these various versions cannot be conflated into one story and reconciled.

We know that Luke had Mark's version of this story available to him. Whether he chose to use Mark's story and change it or whether he had access to yet another story (one, however, that Matthew did not use), we cannot know. We do know that only in his story is the woman a sinner. The emphasis of the story shifts in Luke's version as compared to the others. Here the point becomes not the symbolic action of the anointing, but the pardoning of a great sinner by Jesus.

Ironically, Luke's version has overshadowed that of Mark and Matthew, partly due to Luke's skill as a storyteller, but even more so because that is the version told in the Lectionary (Cycle C, the sixteenth Sunday in Ordinary Time). So it is the only version that we will ever hear proclaimed at Mass. Further, tradition has gone on to erroneously attribute this action to Mary Magdalene, who is not even mentioned in the story. It was the reputation of the woman who was a sinner that associated her with Mary Magdalene from whom seven demons had gone out.

Only in John is the story told of Jesus being anointed by his friend, Mary, the sister of Martha and Lazarus. Here the action is done by a faithful friend and follower expressing her love. Here, too, in keeping with John's focus, the action takes on huge significance as prefiguring the passion ahead.

This background is necessary for clarification before we focus on the story of Mary of Bethany anointing Jesus. The following chart outlines the story of the woman anointing Jesus in all four gospel accounts.

Woman Anoints Jesus

Mark 14:3–9	Matthew 26:6–13	John 12:1–8	Luke 7:36–50
House of Simon the leper in Bethany/ prelude to the passion	House of Simon the leper in Bethany/ prelude to passion	House of Martha and Mary in Bethany/prelude to the passion/after raising of Lazarus	In Galilee during ministry
Unnamed woman	Unnamed woman	Mary of Bethany	"A woman in the city, who was a sinner"
Brings an alabaster jar of expensive ointment and pours it on the head of Jesus, as prophets anoint kings (1 Sam 15:5, 16:13; 1 Kgs 1:45, 19:15–16; 2 Kgs 9:1–13; Dan 9:24).	Brings an alabaster jar of expensive ointment and pours it on the head of Jesus, as prophets anoint kings (1 Sam 15:5, 16:13; 1 Kgs 1:45, 19:15–16; 2 Kgs 9:1–13; Dan 9:24).	Takes a pound of expensive ointment, anoints Jesus' feet, and wipes them with her hair.	Wets Jesus' feet with her tears, wipes them with her hair, kisses his feet, and anoints them with ointment.
Onlookers protest waste. Jesus defends the woman, that the anointing is preparation for his burial.	Disciples protest waste. Jesus defends the woman, that the anointing is embalming for his burial.	Judas protests waste. Jesus defends Mary, that the anointing is preparation for his burial.	Pharisee host objects to "sort of woman" who is touching Jesus. Jesus tells parable of debts forgiven.
Jesus speaks: "Let her alone…wherever the good news is proclaimed in the whole world, what she has done will be told in remembrance of her."	Jesus speaks: "Why do you trouble the woman?…wherever this good news is proclaimed in the whole world, what she has done will be told in remembrance of her."	Jesus speaks: "Leave her alone…"	Jesus speaks: "Her sins, which were many, have been forgiven; hence she has shown great love."
NOT in Lectionary	NOT in Lectionary	NOT in Lectionary	IN Lectionary

REFLECTION QUESTIONS

Scripture readings: Luke 10:38–42; John 11:1–44, 12:1–11

- What questions come to mind as you read Mary's story? Make a note of them to bring to our next gathering.
- Have you ever had the experience, like Mary, of being in a privileged place where you, perhaps, did not belong but where you wanted to be? How did it feel?
- How do you respond in your life to the need for quiet and contemplation? Compare your responses with one another.
- Have you ever imagined yourself at the feet of Jesus? What would that be like?
- Mary only speaks once in all of these passages and it is to repeat the identical words of her sister, "Lord, if you had been here, my brother would not have died." What words would she have chosen for her own gravestone?
- Did it help to sort out the various anointings in scripture? What do you think was the original story or stories? Why?
- Choose five (or more) adjectives to describe Mary's action in anointing Jesus.
- How did you feel about Jesus' words, "Leave her alone..."?

CHALLENGE

Mary, the woman who sat in silence in Luke 10, becomes Mary, the woman who acts prophetically in John 11. How does your prayer life inspire your public life?

MARY OF BETHANY'S PRAYER

Six days before the Passover Jesus came to Bethany, the home of Lazarus, whom he had raised from the dead. There they gave a dinner for him. Martha served, and Lazarus was one of those at the table with him. Mary took a pound of costly perfume made of pure nard, anointed Jesus' feet, and wiped them with her hair. The house was filled with the fragrance of the perfume. But Judas Iscariot, one of his disciples (the one who was about to betray him), said, "Why was this perfume not sold for three hundred denarii and the money given to the poor?" Jesus said, "Leave her alone. She bought it so that she might keep it for the day of my burial. You always have the poor with you, but you do not always have me." (John 12:1–5, 7–8)

Mary, who sat at the feet of Jesus, here stands and, still without words, proclaims her love and her conviction with her actions. Whatever first stirred within her as she earlier listened to her Lord is now fanned into flame in the afterglow of her brother's life being returned to them. Like her sister, Martha, who came to faith in stages, Mary here shows her realization that this man is more than man. She may have loved him before but here she uses the ancient act of anointing to acknowledge that he is priest, prophet, and king. In a way that is significant, perhaps even beyond her realizing it, she points to Jesus' immanent death, burial, and resurrection.

O God of Mary,
You have filled our minds and our hearts
with words, ideas, and hopes that fire our imagination and lift us up.
You have shattered our complacency and preconceived notions.
There is a thirst within us that only you can fill, and we long to quench
*   that thirst,*
to sit in your company for hours on end.
Because of you, we are moved to rise up and become
what we never knew ourselves to be.
Because of you, we can love extravagantly and act boldly.
Emboldened by the knowledge that you will uphold and protect us,

we proclaim with our lives that you are Messiah, the Son of God.
You are our Lord and Savior.
Amen.

A CLOSER LOOK AT THE TEXT

Mary of Bethany, sister of Martha and Lazarus, only speaks one time and repeats the words of her sister, "Lord, if you had been here my brother would not have died" (John 11:32). She is truly one of whom it can be said her actions speak louder than her words. Judas protests that her perfume could have been sold for three hundred silver pieces. That was nearly a year's pay, because each silver piece or denarius was equal to a day's wage. Mary has access to wealth and uses it to express her profound gratitude to and love for this Jesus who has not only returned her brother to her from the dead, but who has also deeply touched and transformed her life. Some conversions are so overwhelming that words are inadequate; only actions springing spontaneously from within can suffice. Her actions are extravagant—"the house was filled with the fragrance of the perfume" (John 12:3b)—and they combine the sensuous expression of great love with the reverent attitude of enacted ritual. She goes beyond an act of gratitude and love for she anoints Jesus' feet. Throughout scripture and Hebrew tradition those who were anointed were priests, prophets, and kings. Here Mary is recognizing and ritually confessing that Jesus is all of these. Yet, she is doing still more. For we know that in John's Gospel, all actions point to the central truths of the incarnation, passion, death, and resurrection. Jesus recognized that Mary's anointing is, in fact, preparation for his own burial.

In a truly prophetic stance Mary unites the past, the present, and the future. She hearkens to the past in enacting Israel's anointing of priests, prophets, and kings. She stands in the present as she expresses her love and gratitude for Jesus, and she prophesies the future as her actions point to the imminent passion and death of Christ.

The anointing of Jesus takes place after the raising of Lazarus and speaks to a profession of faith. Just as Martha's dialogue with Jesus shows how she grew into her great profession of faith, Mary's decisive, public act presents a radically changed Mary from the silent, passive one sitting at his feet. We can only guess how Lazarus's resurrection brought about this remarkable change.

In looking at the fullness of the Martha and Mary story beyond the vignettes and the stereotypes, we can see that the two sisters come full circle in their growth and complement each other.

Martha

Woman of Action	Woman of Faith
Positives: Gifted with hospitality, good with details, food, hearth, and home, welcoming, generous, giving, capable, hard-working, industrious	Christological statement of faith Parallels Peter's confession (e.g., of mature faith)
Negatives: Busy, task-centered	

Mary

Contemplative	Prophet
Positives: Takes time for quiet and nurturing her soul, listening, receiving, accepting, at Christ's feet	Aware, inspired, dramatic, symbolic gesture, ritual enactment, courageous
Negatives: Unaware, passive, not concerned or connected with needs of others	

A WORD ABOUT ALL THOSE MARYS

We recently took a look at Mary, Jesus' mother, and here we have another Mary, Martha's sister, with yet another Mary ahead next week, Mary Magdalene. Let's look at the other Marys mentioned in the Gospels.

Both Mark and Matthew write about a Mary who is identified as the mother of James and sometimes the mother, as well, of Joses (probably meaning Joseph) and Salome and the mother of Zebedee's sons. She can be found "looking on from a distance" at the cross in Mark 15:40 and at the tomb in Mark 15:40, 47 and Matthew 16:1. Matthew 28:1 places "Mary Magdalene and the other Mary" at the tomb. This "other Mary" may or may not be the Mary, mother of James, Joses, and Salome. And John 19:25 adds yet another Mary in his picture of the crucifixion when he writes, "…standing near the cross of Jesus were his mother, and his mother's sister, Mary the wife of Clopas, and Mary Magdalene." So, we have the three Marys of our Bible study: Mary of Nazareth, Mary of Bethany, and Mary Magdalene, but we also have Mary the mother of James (and others), Matthew's "other Mary" (who may or may not be the same as James' mother), and Mary, the wife of Clopas. Just to keep things interesting there is an additional Mary in Acts, "the mother of John whose other name was Mark, [in whose home] many had gathered and were praying" (Acts 12:12).

MARY MAGDALENE

Background

Mary Magdalene or Mary of Magdala is named fourteen times in the Gospels, more than any of the disciples outside of Peter, James, and John. This, of itself, is remarkable when we cannot even get a list of the twelve names of the apostles that "match." (Mark and Matthew list a "Thaddeus" who is, presumably, the same person listed in Luke as "Judas, son of James." John uses the name "Nathaniel" where the Synoptics use "Bartholomew.") Even more important, however, than the frequency with which her name appears, is the time and place of her appearance. All four Gospels place Mary Magdalene at both the crucifixion and the resurrection—the only one so named. This establishes, beyond a doubt, not only her historical presence at these central events in the life of Christ, but it is also an indication of her importance both in the life of the followers of Jesus and in the life of the early Church that recorded these events.

In being sent by Jesus to bear the news of his resurrection (John 20:11–19), Mary becomes the "Apostle to the Apostles"—a phrase first coined by Hippolytus of Rome in the second century. According to *Webster's Dictionary,* the word *apostle* means "one sent on a mission." In these passages, it is Jesus himself who sends her with the most essential mission or message—that he is risen—and he sends her to the most critical of persons—his innermost followers. Apostle is a title of great distinction in the Bible. Paul would later make a great deal of what it means to be an apostle: "Last of all, as to one untimely born, he appeared also to me. For I am the least of the apostles, unfit to be called an apostle, because I persecuted the church of God. But by the grace of God I am what I am, and his grace toward me has not been in vain" (1 Cor 15:8–10), and he would roundly condemn false prophets. But Mary Magdalene lives up to every definition of apostle—be that of Hippolytus, Paul, or *Webster's*. And that claim is based entirely and legitimately on what is found in scripture. She is sent with authority on a mission. She is the first to proclaim the news of the risen Lord. Her news, "I have seen the Lord" (John 20:18), is the central message of Christianity. As Paul would later write, "If Christ has not been raised, then our proclamation has been in vain and your faith has been in vain" (1 Cor 15:14). She is eyewitness to both the risen Christ and the example of his life lived among us.

Without the witness of Mary Magdalene and the other women who stood at the cross and came to the tomb, we would have no first-hand account of Easter. We would not know what happened. Jesus chose to entrust her with the most important of proclamations. In addition to being a witness to the resurrection, Mary Magdalene is a faithful disciple for all the time she spent supporting Jesus throughout his ministry and sharing his life and that of his followers.

REFLECTION QUESTIONS

Scripture readings: Mark 15:40—16:14; Matthew 27:55—28:10;
Luke 8:1–3, 23:44—24:12; John 19:25, 20:1–18

- What questions come to mind as you read Mary's story? Make a note of them to bring to our next gathering.
- Luke 8:1–3 lists Mary among the women accompanying and traveling with Jesus: "Mary, called Magdalene, from whom seven demons had gone out." Make a quick check of some of these other scripture references to demon possession: (a) Matt 8:28–34, Mark 5:1–10, or Luke 8:26–38; (b) Matt 9:32–34; (c) Matt 12:22–24 or Luke 11:14–16; (d) Matt 17:14–18 or Luke 9:37–44; (e) Luke 4:33–37; (f) Matt 15:21–28 or Mark 7:24–30. Are any of these possessions associated with sinfulness?
- Using the blank chart provided (p. 96), make notes of how the four evangelists record the events of the crucifixion and the resurrection. Circle any significant details or differences. Use the space at the bottom to record phrases that stand out for you. What questions, if any, does this raise for you?
- Only in John's Gospel do we have the touching scene between Mary and Jesus in the garden. What details of that scene touch your imagination? Raise questions for you?
- In John 20:11–18, Mary encounters the risen Lord. She is sent to announce to the others that Jesus has risen from the dead. St. Augustine in the fourth century wrote of Mary Magdalene, "The Holy Spirit made Magdalene the Apostle of the Apostles." Is that how you have commonly thought of or pictured Mary Magdalene? If so, why?

	Who is at the cross? Where?	Who is at the burial?	Who goes to the tomb?	What do they see there?
Matthew				
Mark				
Luke				
John				

CHALLENGE

Mary is confused about whom she encounters in the garden, thinking Jesus is the gardener. Then he calls her by name and she recognizes him. Is there a time in your life when, out of the confusion, you have heard Jesus call you by name? What moved within you? What was your response?

MARY MAGDALENE'S PRAYER

But Mary stood weeping outside the tomb. As she wept, she bent over to look into the tomb; and she saw two angels in white, sitting where the body of Jesus had been lying, one at the head and the other at the feet. They said to her, "Woman, why are you weeping?" She said to them, "They have taken away my Lord, and I do not know where they have laid him." When she had said this, she turned around and saw Jesus standing there, but she did not know that it was Jesus. Jesus said to her, "Woman, why are you weeping? Whom are you looking for?" Supposing him to be the gardener, she said to him, "Sir, if you have carried him away, tell me where you have laid him, and I will take him away." Jesus said to her, "Mary!" She turned and said to him in Hebrew, "Rabbouni!" (which means Teacher). Jesus said to her, "Do not hold on to me, because I have not yet ascended to the Father. But go to my brothers and say to them, 'I am ascending to my Father and your Father, to my God and your God.'" Mary Magdalene went and announced to the disciples, "I have seen the Lord"; and she told them that he had said these things to her. (John 20:11–18)

Mary's grief compelled her to return to the tomb early that morning after observing the Sabbath. The grip of that same grief prevented her from recognizing Jesus even though he stood before her. It was only when he spoke her name that her grief was shattered and she became aware that he was truly present and alive. In that moment she was caught between the familiarity of his voice, his nearness, the sound of her name, and the shock and astonishment of his being truly alive—for she herself had witnessed the fullness of his suffering, the finality of his death. Only the intimacy of her own name spoken by that well-known voice allowed her to overcome the memory of all that she had witnessed and believe what stood before her.

Rabbouni,
you call us by our name
and our hearts leap within us.
Can it be that you are alive—so close, so real?
Darkness and death are scattered in the light of your being
and we dare to believe.
We want to hold this moment, hold you forever.
Yet you would have us carry our new-found belief to others.
It is your trust in us that sends us in your name.
We bear the news that you are alive!

That everything is now changed and made new in you.
We cannot contain it!
The joy spills and spirals out until we hear our own words echoing back,
"I have seen the Lord!"
May our lives proclaim to all whom we meet that you are alive
and in our midst.
Amen.

A CLOSER LOOK AT THE TEXT

So far we have looked only to the Gospels for our information on Mary Magdalene. How do we account for the other images of her? She has been portrayed frequently in the past as a great sinner—standing in scarlet contrast, as it were, to the virginal blue of Mary, Jesus' mother. More recently she has taken center stage in *The Da Vinci Code* and popular lore as the wife or paramour of Jesus. How did all this happen? Who was she really?

Although the early Church fathers frequently extolled the virtues of Mary Magdalene, over time a different picture of her emerged. Some of this can be attributed to confusion over the several Marys and other women of the Gospels, and the resulting tendency to conflate these into one. Over time, the dominant image associated with Mary Magdalene became that of a repentant sinner. In AD 590, Pope Gregory the Great preached a homily in which he combined the woman who anointed Jesus in Luke's Gospel with Mary of Bethany and Mary Magdalene. Using the technique of allegory common among the Church fathers at that time, he equated the seven demons that Jesus drove out of Mary (Luke 8:2) with the seven deadly sins and said, "She whom Luke calls the sinful woman, whom John calls Mary, we believe to be the Mary from whom seven devils were ejected according to Mark. And what did these seven devils signify, if not all the vices?" (Gregory the Great, Homily 33). She thus became a model of repentance and was actually named the "Patron Saint of Prostitutes." Although some writers, including the German nun Anne Catharine Emmerich (1774–1824), have made much of exploiting the salaciousness of this image, other writers and artists, such as the great eleventh-century theologian and saint Anselm of Canterbury, have found much comfort and encouragement in the still-popular image of Mary Magdalene as repentant sinner.

Impetus for the recovery of Mary Magdalene's prominent role in the early Christian community was given in part by the rather recent rediscovery of old manuscripts. The Dead Sea Scrolls were discovered in Israel in 1947. Two years earlier, in 1945, near Nag Hammadi in upper Egypt, a similar cache of texts was found that dated back to a somewhat later period in the early Christian era; these are commonly referred to as *Gnostic Gospels.* Although the writings at Nag Hammadi were not the only extant Gnostic Gospels, they were extensive and well preserved. They also brought to public awareness the existence of other noncanonical or apocryphal Gospels written about Christ. These Gospels contain intriguing passages about Mary Magdalene that portray her as favored by Jesus, as a leader in the early Church, and as one in conflict with Peter. Thus they provide the basis for the recent upsurge of interest in and speculation about Mary Magdalene.

Whereas these writings appear to shed fascinating light on the life of Christianity in its early, formative stages (the apocryphal Gospel of Thomas contains sayings of Jesus that may well be authentic), they were not included in the New Testament canon because they did not successfully meet the criteria for acceptance. These criteria were: (1) a work had to be reasonably regarded as having apostolic origins, real or reputed; (2) it had to have been addressed to and preserved by a particular Christian community; and (3) it had to conform to the rule of faith, reflecting the beliefs of the earliest Christians. The most striking difference between the canonical Gospels and the apocryphal and Gnostic Gospels is that the former are named for their presumed author and thus indicate the community in which they originated, and they focus on Jesus; the latter are named for another figure from the life of Jesus, and they focus on that figure. Also, for the most part these Gospels were written after (sometimes well after) the canonical Gospels and thus do not have apostolicity or antiquity on their side.

Thanks to recent advances in biblical scholarship and knowledge of the early Christian world, the image of Mary Magdalene as Apostle to the Apostles and leader in the early Church has been recovered without having to rely on apocryphal writings. From the pages of the Gospels there arises the powerful witness of a remarkable woman of faith, a partner with Jesus in the good news and the herald of the resurrection.

Woman at the Well

Background

Only in John's Gospel do we find mention of Jesus' ministry among the Samaritans. Jesus decides to return to Galilee from Judea because the Pharisees now turn their attention from John the Baptist to him. The most direct route, a three-day journey, passes through the territory of the Samaritans, who were often hostile to the Jews. In the Greek manuscripts the town is referred to as Sychari, which is thought to be a corruption of Sychem or Shechem. Some translations use the name Askar, which is the name of the town in that area today. There is no doubt about the location of Jacob's well, just outside of Askar. The Book of Joshua records, "The bones of Joseph, which the Israelites had brought up from Egypt, were buried at Shechem, in the portion of ground that Jacob had bought from the children of Hamor, the father of Shechem, for one hundred pieces of money; it became an inheritance of the descendants of Joseph" (Josh 24:32). This well is a sacred place to all the descendants of Jacob and Joseph, but is held in especially high regard by the Samaritans on whose land it is and who are not ritually connected with worship at the temple in Jerusalem.

It is unheard of for a rabbi to speak familiarly with a woman in public and also for a Jew to ask for water from a Samaritan. Jews considered the Samaritans and, therefore, their utensils for eating and drinking to be unclean. Jesus shows, however, in other pericopes that he is not troubled by such taboos. He speaks favorably of Samaritans in other places, such as in the parable of the Good Samaritan (Luke 10:25–37) and the episode of the healing of the ten lepers (Luke 17:11–19). The Gospels frequently record his enlightened attitude toward women.

John makes use of dialogues in his Gospel to provide revelations about Jesus. In these there is the pairing of Jesus as the protagonist with another who asks the questions. There is a third party, unnamed but present as well, in the readers or hearers of the dialogue who are aware of the ironies and double meanings within the language and images. Some of the most important of these dialogues are between Jesus and Nicodemus (John 3:1–21), Jesus and the Samaritan woman (John 4:1–42), and the one with Martha of Bethany (John 11:1–44). The conversation with the

Samaritan woman follows closely after the one with Nicodemus and is intended to reinforce and contrast with that. The noontime encounter, for example, contrasts with Nicodemus' nighttime encounter. Where Nicodemus came by night and left in the dark, this conversation occurs when the sun is at its zenith.

REFLECTION QUESTIONS

Scripture readings: John 4:1–42

- What questions come to mind as you read this story? Make a note of them to bring to our next gathering.
- Look at this long discourse as a series of exchanges between Jesus and the woman:

(A) **Verses 7–9**

Context: This dialogue stands alongside the one with Nicodemus (John 3:1–21) with the intervening space given over to John the Baptist and baptism. In the opening verses, we move immediately to water. What does this tell you?

Setting: What have we learned about the significance of a man meeting a woman at a well?

In response to Jesus' request for water, the woman asks him a significant, forthright question: "How is it that you, a Jew, ask a drink of me, a woman of Samaria?" How does her frankness invite Jesus' disclosure?

(B) **Verses 10–12**

Jesus shifts the focus of the conversation to his own identity and makes the offer of living water as opposed to cistern water. While still thinking only in terms of moving (living) versus still water, the woman picks up on his shift to identity and asks if he is greater than "our ancestor Jacob" (note they share this ancestor)—another major question. What ironies and symbols in this exchange would John's readers pick up on?

(C) **Verses 13–15**

Jesus elaborates on the living water as welling from within and providing eternal life. Not yet fully aware of the implications, the woman, nonetheless, responds with immediate desire for this offering. Again, her readiness invites Jesus to reveal his meaning further. See Isaiah 55:1–3 and compare it to Jesus' offer.

(D) Verses 16–17a and (E) Verses 17b–20

With this set of exchanges the conversation seems to take a turn. What do you think it is about? Do you see any reference to sin or shame? Does she express repentance? Does Jesus forgive or warn against sinning again? Why or why not? Can you think of any explanation from within the Jewish laws on marriage that would explain her situation?

The turn in this conversation seems to open her eyes to the hidden meaning in what Jesus is saying. The woman immediately points out that which theologically divides the Jews and the Samaritans. Again she opens the door for Jesus to explain further.

(F) Verses 21–26

Jesus responds to her with a long discourse on authentic worship that transcends the worship of both the Samaritans and the Jews. How would John's readers hear these verses?

Like Martha and Mary, who come to faith by stages, the woman now introduces the concept of the Messiah. In Jesus' simple response, "I am he, the one who is speaking to you," we have the admission by Jesus of his identity. Where else have you heard "I am..."?

(G) The aftermath, Verses 27–42

The authenticity of her conversion is played out by her dropping everything and running to proclaim her discovery. Her testimony is compelling enough to bring others to Jesus, who, in turn, prevail upon him to stay for two days. In the end they are able to say, "It is no longer because of what you said that we believe, for we have heard for ourselves, and we know that this is truly the Savior of the world" (verse 42).

From whom have you heard of Jesus in such a compelling way?

- When were you able to say as an adult, "I believe not because of what others have told me but because I've come to know Jesus myself"?
- What characterizes a good evangelist? Do you possess some of those qualities?

- Whom do you see in your life or community that has those qualities?
- What does it tell you about the community to whom John was writing that he has two women as the central characters who evangelize—this pericope and Mary Magdalene in 20:11–18? What does it say to you today?
- The other women who were paired in our study actually encountered each other; these two women, Mary Magdalene and the Woman at the Well, do not. Why do you think they might be paired together? What do they have in common? Are they are a suitable match for one another? Why or why not?

CHALLENGE

How do I feel about the way this woman and her "sister" Mary Magdalene have had such negative reputations? Does this call forth any response in me?

Space for your own reflections

PRAYER OF THE WOMAN AT THE WELL

Many Samaritans from that city believed in him because of the woman's testimony, "He told me everything I have ever done." So when the Samaritans came to him, they asked him to stay with them; and he stayed there two days. And many more believed because of his word. They said to the woman, "It is no longer because of what you said that we believe, for we have heard for ourselves, and we know that this is truly the Savior of the world." (John 4:39–42)

Jesus chooses to reveal his identity to the Samaritan woman. Their conversation is a profound theological discussion in which she fully participates. The open honesty of her questions and response invite Jesus to deeper and deeper revelation. When at last she comes to understanding, she drops everything and runs to share with others what she has learned. Because of her conviction and the authenticity of her words, others come to Jesus and to belief.

Give us to drink,
God of the Living Water,
that we will never thirst again.
Fountain of Eternal Life, spring fresh within us—
a stream flowing from our baptism.
May the Living Water we carry pour out to others.
May our lives and words so mirror their Source
that others will come to drink as well.
May they come to know for themselves
that you truly the Savior of the World.
Amen.

A CLOSER LOOK AT THE TEXT

Here we will offer a feminist interpretation of John 4:1–42 as put forward by Sandra M. Schneiders, professor of New Testament Studies and Christian Spirituality at the Jesuit School of Theology and the Graduate Theological Union in Berkeley, CA, in *The Revelatory Text.* This is not offered as the definitive explanation of what this text represents. Rather, it offers an alternate understanding that (1) exemplifies the methods of feminist criticism and (2) stands in contrast to previous interpretations.

Feminist criticism is just one form of biblical criticism. Already we have looked at methods such as *form criticism,* which identifies the type of genre being read and its literary context, and *historical criticism,* which considers the social, political, and historical setting of both the text and the author. Feminist criticism uses the full range of biblical scholarship tools but does so with the approach that the biblical text, and its interpretation over the centuries, contains an *androcentric* (male-centered) bias. The purpose, therefore, is to uncover the bias to better arrive at the underlying meaning of the text.

The Bible, like any written text, is not neutral. Although inspired by God, it still has human authors who chose what to include, what not to include, as well as how to say it. Additionally, until very recently, all those persons who have interpreted the meaning of scriptures—virtually all biblical scholars, pastors, and homilists—have been men who themselves have received training and instruction from men within a society and an ecclesial culture that was male dominated. Given that, there is a certain incapacity for them to view things other than as men with the built-in partiality that entails. Though a feminist critique has its bias as well, by offering a different lens through which to view the scriptures, it can sometimes serve as an alternative or a healthy corrective.

First, Schneiders invites us to look at both historical and literary presuppositions. Historically, she places the authorship of the Woman at the Well pericope within the Johannine community—the early Christian community that gathered around the beloved disciple—and suggests that it was written to address the tension that existed between Samaritan Christians and Jewish Christians in the early Church. Thus, the theological issues that divided the two groups are addressed and resolved in the conversation. Jewish legitimacy is reaffirmed but the validity of Samaritan faith tradition is also honored, despite the history of infidelity among the

Samaritans. Both traditions, however, give way to an "hour [that] is coming when you will worship the Father neither on this mountain nor in Jerusalem" (John 4:21).

Taking a close look at the literary form, Schneiders first points out the significance of its being a *type story,* that is, one that follows the recognized biblical pattern of a man meeting a woman at a well: Abraham's servant finding Rebecca (Gen 24:10–61), Jacob meeting Rachel (Gen 29:1–20), and Moses receiving Zipporah (Exod 2:16–22). Additionally, Jesus has already been cast as the bridegroom twice in John in episodes just preceding this one: at the wedding at Cana (2:9–10) and by John the Baptist (3:27–30). All of this alerts the reader to what is coming and sets the foundation for an encounter that has extraordinary implications.

Another important literary notation that Schneiders makes is that this pericope must be seen within its larger context of John (chapters 2 to 4), the Cana to Cana section—beginning with the wedding at Cana and ending with the royal official's son in Cana. There is a progression of faith within these chapters. At the start, the disciples of Jesus come to belief because of his miracle; at the end a non-Jew comes to belief because of Jesus' word. Within those chapters are two great discourses or conversations that reveal who Jesus is. One is with Nicodemus (3:1–15), who comes in the night and whose belief at the end is not explicit. (Later in John 7:50 we find he "was one of them" and he appears again at the burial in John 19:39.) The other is the Samaritan woman, who encounters Jesus in midday and who not only comes to believe, but who brings her whole town to belief. Schneiders sees the placement of the Samaritan woman between Nicodemus and the royal official as another clue to her significance. She becomes a representative figure or symbolic character—not only of Samaria, but also of the New Israel who is given to Jesus the Bridegroom.

Perhaps the most noteworthy contribution of Schneiders in this interpretation is the close look that she gives to the conversation itself. From the beginning, the Samaritan woman focuses on religious, even theological, themes. First she asks him why he breaks with Jewish tradition in asking her for a drink. When Jesus offers living water, she questions his implication that he is on a par with Jacob, a patriarch whom they both share. This question typifies Samaritan theology that focused on Moses and the patriarchs as opposed to David and the monarchy, which were more important in the Jewish tradition. The Samaritans did not believe that the messiah would be a descendant of David but, rather, that he would be a prophet like Moses (as promised in Deut 18:18–19) and that when he came he would reveal all things and restore true worship—worship that, according to Samaritans, would rightfully take place in the northern kingdom, not in Jerusalem. How specific and theologically probing her words then become with this interpretation: "I see that you are a prophet. Our ancestors worshiped on this mountain, but you say that the place where people must worship is Jerusalem....I know that Messiah is coming. When he comes, he will proclaim all things to us" (John 4:19, 20, 25).

In Schneiders's interpretation, the exchange in midconversation about the five husbands is neither an aside nor a prelude to the theological discussion. It is at the heart of it, if we catch the symbolic importance: (1) This is a type story with bride/bridegroom symbolism and language, (2) the woman is a representative character, and (3) in prophetic literature adultery and idolatry are virtually synonymous. With this understanding, the woman then represents Samaria, and her "five husbands" are the false gods of the five foreign tribes that the Samaritans' ancestors fell into worshipping after their remnants returned from Assyria (2 Kgs 17:13–34). And the "husband" she has now, the God of the covenant, is not truly her husband in the full integrity of covenant as the Jews would know it.

Schneiders sums it up nicely:

> The entire dialogue between Jesus and the woman is the "wooing" of Samaria to full covenant fidelity in the New Israel by Jesus, the New Bridegroom. It has nothing to do with the woman's private moral life but with the covenant life of the community. Nowhere in the fourth gospel is there a dialogue of such theological depth and intensity....In this scene the woman is not simply a "foil" feeding Jesus cue lines. She is a genuine theological dialogue partner gradually experiencing Jesus' self revelation even as she reveals herself to him. (p. 191)

Schneiders's interpretation exists as one among many and is not offered as something one must believe, but it stands in marked contrast to the usual renderings of this gospel passage. Certainly, it undermines an interpretation that would cast the Samaritan woman as yet another immoral woman, one that Jesus cleverly tricks into exposing her sinful past. Perhaps the take-away from all of this is not that Schneiders's interpretation is the correct one but, simply, that we cannot assume that the traditional one is the correct one.

Hopefully as we come to the close of *Sisters in Scripture* we have learned a new respect for the Bible: that it may mean even more than we had ever guessed and that it is permissible, even good, to ask questions and learn new ways to uncover meaning. Hopefully, we've seen how our own experience of scripture and prayer is expanded and enhanced by the company of trusted others. Last, we hope that the initial attraction that the Bible held for us has increased with this study and that we have grown in our attentiveness to God's whisperings in our lives—through scripture, prayer, the stories of one another, and all of our life experience.

God bless you.

CLOSING SESSION

The Closing Session contains four elements: (1) Women Wisdom: sharing on the sister in scripture that each woman has chosen, (2) quiet reflection/journaling time and then sharing with one another, (3) a meal together, and (4) an affirmation exercise. (See sample timeline on p. 112.) The evening session begins with the meal; an afternoon session may do the same. The sample timelines are suggestions; feel free to create an agenda and flow that suits your group.

Preparation: Women Wisdom

For the previous session, prepare slips of paper with all the names of the women discussed during the course: Sarah, Hagar, Rebecca, Rachel, Leah, Ruth, Naomi, Elizabeth, Mary of Nazareth, Martha of Bethany, Mary of Bethany, Mary Magdalene, and the Woman at the Well (see sample text in the box on p. 111). Then ask each participant to draw one of the names from a bowl or basket at that session and to come to the closing session prepared to share something on that woman. The women should be given the freedom to create whatever they choose—a simple sharing of what they learned, a letter to that woman in scripture, a midrash, a poem, a collage, a picture, music—the possibilities are endless.

After the initial welcoming and settling in, invite each woman to share who her character is and what she came up with for that sister in scripture. Following the usual guidelines for sharing, everyone participates.

Guided Reflection Questions

Give each woman some paper to write on and ask them to reflect on the following questions: "What have I learned about myself and about God through this study? How is God calling me in my life now?" After an allotted time of up to fifteen minutes, participants are asked to turn to one other person and share their responses.

Meal Together

It's nice if the components of the meal are shared by all participants. A simple potluck is appropriate, or a salad bar in which each person signs up to bring something on a list (e.g., mixed greens, chopped tomatoes, dressing, rolls and butter, etc.), or a taco bar (e.g., taco meat, beans, shredded cheese, tortilla chips, sour cream, etc.).

After the sharing, take time to lay out the components of your meal together and continue informal conversation over the food.

Affirmation Exercise

The group should move to a setting where there is a comfortable, central chair and other seating around it. Place a small table in front of the chair. On the table place an assortment of small rocks or other similar items—wooden hearts, shells—with one word written on each one. Words to inscribe might include: wisdom, courage, humor, joy, peace, beauty, love, encouragement, strength, compassion, faith, hope, truth, balance, leadership, energy, tranquility, gentleness. Several should also be blank for people to use for other attributes. Also place a large shallow bowl or basket on the table.

Each woman takes a turn in the central chair and the other women go around selecting, in turn, a stone to give to the one in the chair. The woman giving the stone explains how this particular attribute describes the other woman as she places it into her hand. The woman in the chair holds the received stone in her hand for a moment and then places the stone in the bowl. The blank stones can be used for attributes not listed or for repeating one already used.

You may want to close with one last squeeze prayer, Our Father, or a song or dance.

SISTERS IN SCRIPTURE

In preparation for our time together at our closing retreat, we will pray and ask the Holy Spirit's guidance and then each woman will draw the name of one of our sisters in Scripture. The woman you are asked to reflect upon is: _____.

Please spend some time this week prayerfully reflecting on what our study of this woman has taught you and how it has touched your life. You may want to create a midrash, poem, letter, collage, or drawing to share with the other women when we come together. You may want to bring a symbol that represents this woman to you. Be creative and trust God to surprise you.

SUGGESTED SCHEDULES FOR CLOSING SESSION

Morning

9:30   Gather, welcome, settle in

9:45   Opening prayer/song

9:50   Share Women Wisdom

10:45 Quiet time with Reflection Questions:

What have I learned about myself and about God through this study?

How is God calling me in my life right now?

11:00 Sharing in pairs on Reflection Questions

11:30 Lunch

12:00 Affirmation Exercise

12:45 Closing prayer/song

Afternoon or Evening

(Times given in parentheses are for an evening session.)

12:30 (6:30) Gather, welcome, settle in

12:45 (6:45) Lunch or dinner

1:10 (7:10) Opening prayer/song—God of Day and God of Darkness

1:15 (7:15) Share Women Wisdom

1:50 (7:50) Quiet time with Reflection Questions:

What have I learned about myself and about God through this study?

How is God calling me in my life right now?

2:00 (8:00) Sharing in pairs on Reflection Questions

2:15 (8:15) Affirmation Exercise

2:55 (8:55) Closing prayer/song

Appendix: Sample Midrashes

Sarah

Not sure why we have to leave our home. Now we have no food after wandering from place to place. To whom is my husband listening? Is he crazy? Is he ashamed of me to not even treat me as a wife but to give me to Pharaoh? I am not worthy because I have not been able to carry a baby to term. I wonder if he will leave me here in Egypt.

Leah on the Roof

(To the tune of "If I Were a Rich Man")
If I were a rich girl,
I would still be only property for men!
Bargained for as though I were a slave,
Useful at the stove and in the tent!

But if I were a beauty,
Then perhaps I'd be the storyteller's prize!
To sing my praises through the age to come,
A famous, "favored" wife in history's eyes!

Naomi

The Land remembers me, for

Dust whence all my peoples came
Curled through the toes my sandals trod.

Familiar scents in smoke and winds
Oft carried whispers from my God.

I hunger for tastes of familiar foods;
The preparing of them in certain ways
Not known here; or cast aside—
Impossible even, by vendors' displays.

The well grants more than sufficiency here,
But ever so slightly bitter it seems.
Families are kind through invisible walls
Laid silently down with customs and means.

I fear now, walking these hills alone,
A stranger without joy of well-loved faces,
For talking and laughter; most gone now.
But remembered. In dreamed places.

And so it pulls, it tugs, it calls…
By whatever means can be,
I long to return to where
The Land remembers me.

Elizabeth

Lord God, I don't understand. What's with you giving these older women babies? It takes a lot of energy to keep up with a toddler. And poor Zechariah. I admit it is a relief to have him speechless at times, but don't you think this is a bit extreme? I mean, can you blame him for doubting? I am not a young woman anymore.

And John! Where did you ever come up with a name like that? We have no relatives named John.

Poor Mary. She came to see me. She didn't know how to tell her mother. And your angels were a little late in informing Joseph. If they had told him before, it would have saved both of them a lot of grief. Joseph was ready to divorce her, you know.

But now that I have complained, I just want to tell you that when Mary came to see me, I think my little John started dancing! I could feel him leap for joy. So forgive me for complaining. You have led the People of Israel in ways that we do not understand. So, again we place our trust in you.

Woman at the Well

I am Hannah and I have a most interesting story to tell.

Long ago, at a time when Jews and Samaritans worshiped God differently and did not get along with each other, an itinerant rabbi came to the town of Shechem, the site of Jacob's well. It was about noon and Jesus, the rabbi, sent his disciples to buy provisions. Being tired, he sat down and rested at the well. A Samaritan woman, we will call her Noname, came to draw water, and Jesus asked her for a drink. The woman was surprised that a Jew would ask her, a Samaritan and a woman, for water. Jesus told her that if she knew who it was that was asking for water, she would have asked for water that gives life. Noname was perplexed and asked many questions about where and how to worship. Noname said to Jesus, "I know there is a Messiah coming and he will answer all my questions." Jesus told her that he was the Messiah. She was not embarrassed or afraid, but she was very puzzled. Jesus talked about her life and the woman was amazed that this man knew all about her.

The disciples of Jesus returned and were surprised to see Jesus speaking to a woman, because women were not considered to have much value. Noname ran off into town to invite the people to come and meet someone who was able to tell her everything that she ever did. "He is a prophet," she said, because Samaritans thought that the Messiah would come as a prophet, and she thought that he was the Messiah. The townspeople came to hear him; they were enthralled and asked him to stay for a time. Jesus spent two days with them, and many put their faith in him because of what they heard him say. They came to believe that he was indeed the Messiah—the Savior of the world.

Such an amazing story is this. It was unlikely that a rabbi would speak to a Samaritan, but inconceivable that he spoke to a Samaritan woman. Is this a true story? You must decide for yourself. Some say that it is a completely true story; others believe there are hidden meanings in the story. There are many questions that have not been answered to everyone's satisfaction. Was he the Messiah? A prophet? Did people continue to believe in him? Why did he talk to a woman? You have to judge for yourself.

What do I think? Well, I believe in Jesus, and there are many people who still believe in this Jesus. They are called Christians and they live all over the world: in Jerusalem, Samaria, Rome, in places that we have never heard of. It is all very strange, yet wonderful. Something that happened so long ago still fills people with hope and joy and peace. Don't you feel it?

RESOURCES

Boadt, Lawrence. *Reading the Old Testament: An Introduction.* Mahwah, NJ: Paulist Press, 1984.

Dresner, Samuel H. *Rachel.* Minneapolis, MN: Augsburg Fortress, 1994.

Hebblethwaite, Margaret. *Six New Gospels: New Testament Women Tell Their Stories.* London: Geoffrey Chapman; Boston: Cowley Publications, 1994.

McKenna, Megan. *Leave Her Alone.* Maryknoll, NY: Orbis Books, 2000.

New Jerome Biblical Commentary. Edited by Raymond E. Brown, SS, Joseph A. Fitzmyer, SJ, and Roland E. Murphy, OCarm. Englewood Cliffs, NJ: Prentice-Hall, 1990. Sections on Canonicity, §§66:48–101.

Schneiders, Sandra M. *The Revelatory Text.* New York: HarperSanFranciso, 1991.

Teresa of Avila. *The Interior Castle.* Classics of Western Spirituality. Translated by Kieran Kavanaugh, OCD, and Otilio Rodgriguez, OCD. Mahwah, NJ: Paulist Press, 1979.

Vatican II documents accessible at http://www.vatican.va/archive/hist_councils/ii_vatican_council.

EVALUATION FORM—
SISTERS IN SCRIPTURE

I participated in the:

_____ Morning session of *Sisters in Scripture*

_____ Evening session of *Sisters in Scripture*

I was able to attend:

_____ All the sessions

_____ All the sessions except: _____

_____ I joined late at session: _____

The reason I came was: _____

_____

_____

My previous experience with bible studies was:_____

_____

I found the introductory material to be:

_____ Helpful

_____ Adequate

_____ Somewhat confusing

_____ Overwhelming

Did the layout of the course, the handouts, the schedule, work for you?
Why or why not? _____

_____

_____

Continued

At-Home Experience

My routine for studying the scripture became: _____
_____
_____

Did the background on each woman help you? _____

Please describe your experience of responding to the Reflection Questions.
_____
_____
_____

Were the Reflection Questions helpful to you in finding more meaning in the text? Why or why not?
_____

Did you use the CHALLENGE questions? _____

If you did, which ones and what difference did it make in your faith life?
_____
_____
_____

If not, why not? _____

Did you find the written prayer for each session helpful? _____
_____

Did you create a midrash? _____

If yes, on whom? How did you go about it? How did it feel to do it? What difference, if any, did it make in appreciating, understanding the text?
_____
_____

If not, why not? _____

What advice or comments do you have about the work you did at home in preparation? _____
_____
_____

Continued

Small-Group Experience

Please rate the following on a scale of 1 to 5, with 5 being the highest:

I felt comfortable in my small group.

1_____ 2_____ 3_____ 4_____ 5_____

The facilitator did a good job guiding us through the questions.

1_____ 2_____ 3_____ 4_____ 5_____

The extroverts and introverts balanced out and everyone shared fairly equally.

1_____ 2_____ 3_____ 4_____ 5_____

I liked having open seating where we could sit wherever we liked.

1_____ 2_____ 3_____ 4_____ 5_____

I ended up in one group and preferred to stay there.

1_____ 2_____ 3_____ 4_____ 5_____

The level of sharing in our group was deep and personal.

1_____ 2_____ 3_____ 4_____ 5_____

I found my own faith enriched by the faith of these other women.

1_____ 2_____ 3_____ 4_____ 5_____

Continued

A Closer Look at the Text

How did you feel about using the tools of biblical scholarship to "break open the text"?_____

_____

_____

What advice or comments do you have for the facilitator about the "A Closer Look at the Text" sections or teaching portion of each gathering?

_____

_____

Do you think *Sisters in Scripture* impacted your faith life? If so, please describe:

_____

_____

Did *Sisters in Scripture* enrich your understanding of the Bible? If so, please describe: _____

_____

_____

One thing I will take away from *Sisters in Scripture* is: _____

_____

_____

Something I'd suggest for our second session would be:

_____

_____

Other comments? _____

_____

_____

Name *(optional)*: _____

_____

_____